INTERMEDIATE ARABIC WORKBOOK

FOR REVISION AND PRACTICE

JOHN MACE

تمارين متوسطة في العربية

HIPPOCRENE BOOKS, INC
NEW YORK

Other titles by John Mace:

Basic Arabic Workbook
Arabic Verbs
Arabic For Today: A Student, Business and Professional Course in Spoken and Written Arabic
Arabic Grammar: A Revision and Reference Guide (3rd edition)
Teach Yourself Arabic Verbs
Teach Yourself Arabic Script (2nd edition)
Persian Grammar: For Revision and Reference

Typeset by John Mace

ISBN-13: 978-0-7818-1177-4
ISBN-10: 0-7818-1177-5

For information, address:
HIPPOCRENE BOOKS, INC.
171 Madison Avenue
Suite 1602
New York, NY 10016
www.hippocrenebooks.com

Cataloging-in-Publication data available from the Library of Congress.

Printed in the United States of America

Contents

CONTENTS

Introduction

This *Intermediate Arabic Workbook* is intended as a sequel to the *Basic Arabic Workbook*; the two books have the same purpose and format. Most of the Introduction to the *Basic* book is valid here also.

In the *Basic* book you will have revised, consolidated and exercised the essential elements and patterns of the practical Arabic of today. This *Intermediate* book explores further word- and sentence-structures to make your Arabic more varied and more expressive. As before, the emphasis is on practical use in a working environment; the vocabulary is expanded to 2,100 words in a variety of domains ranging from the community to computing.

In the text, references preceded by the abbreviation 'B' are to chapters (or the Appendix) of the *Basic Arabic Workbook.*

The *Basic* book introduced real-life text in the form of a few short adapted extracts from the Arabic press. This *Intermediate* book includes a greater number and variety of real-life items, all without simplification, from varied sources.

The level of knowledge also permits exercises with activities such as filling in forms, interpreting charts and statistical tables, writing letters, and seeking and recording information.

You should note that throughout the exercises, nouns and adjectives are in the nominative case unless otherwise indicated or necessitated.

I am especially grateful to the following authorities for their kind permission to reproduce very useful material held under their copyright:

- *Al-Arab* newspaper for the extracts from articles reprinted on pages 26 and 72
- *Al-Hayat* newspaper for the extracts from articles reprinted on pages 32, 64 and 86
- the Ministry of the Interior of the United Arab Emirates for the

visa application form reprinted on page 65

- the Arab Bank for Economic Development in Africa (BADEA) for the passage reprinted on page 79
- the Arabic Service of the British Broadcasting Corporation (BBC) for the passage reprinted on page 90
- Bayerische Motorenwerke (BMW) for the passage reprinted on page 104
- the Commercial Bank of Kuwait for the passage reprinted on page 114
- the United Nations Educational, Social and Cultural Organisation (UNESCO), more especially the UNESCO Institute for Statistics (UIS), for the table reprinted on page 115.

My sincere thanks also go to Nicholas Awde and to Marilyn Moore for their proofreading. Any remaining errors are my responsibility.

1 Reading and Writing

- *ruq'a* writing

1. رقعة *ruq'a* script

We examine here the very common educated form of handwriting known as رقعة *ruq'a*. Compare *ruq'a* with standard print:

ا آ أ إ بب ت جج خ د ر سس ش صص ض ط عع غ فف ف
قق ق كي ك كا كل كلا لل ل لا مم م ن ههه ة و ؤ ى ئ ء

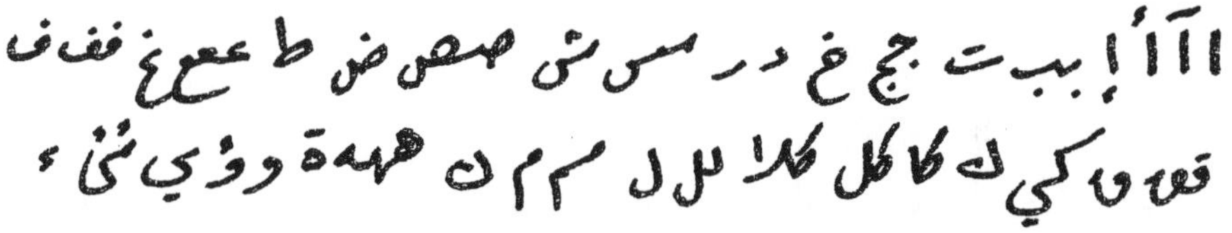

All the handwritten forms shown in the *Basic Arabic Workbook*, Chapter 1 (B 1), are used in *ruq'a*, with the following additions or variants:

- Final/isolated ش , ض and ق are written  :

جيش  جيوش 

بعض  فاض 

عميق  سوق 

and final/isolated ن has the additional common form  :

سابقين 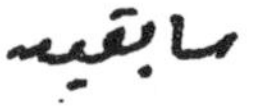 سابقون 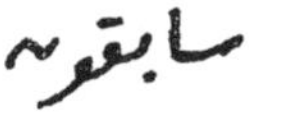

- لا\لا *lām-'alif* is flatter:

لا  بلاد 

- Note the initial, isolated and middle/final forms of the ج group:

خروج  يحتجّ 

Remember that in all print and handwriting you will often find:

- omission of initial *hamza*: ا for initial أ or إ ,
- omission of *tanwīn*: ا\ة\ى for اً\ةً\ىً, and e.g. فاض for فاضٍ ,
- ى (undotted) for both ى (*'alif maqṣura*) and final/isolated ي ,
- omission of *shadda*: e.g. معلم for معلّم .

ruq'a is a prestigious form of handwriting. It is important to be able to read it.

2. رقعة *ruq'a* in print

ruq'a is imitated, with certain variations, in print. Compare standard print, handwritten *ruq'a* and printed *ruq'a*:

قد أخبرنا مشرف النوبة الصباحية من أوّل أمس يوم الثلاثاء الثامن من مارس بأنّك كنت غائبًا دون إجازة عن وظيفتك في قسم الهندسة بين الساعة التاسعة والساعة العاشرة تقريبًا في اليوم المذكور.

قد اخبرنا مشرف النوبة الصباحية من اول امس
يوم الثلاثاء الثامن من مارس بأنك كنت غائبا دون اجازة عن
وظيفتك في قسم الهندسة بين الساعة التاسعة
والساعة العاشرة تقريبا في اليوم المذكور.

قد اخبرنا مشرف النوبة الصباحية من اول امس يوم الثلاثاء الثامن من
مارس بأنك كنت غائبا دون اجازة عن وظيفتك في قسم الهندسة بين
الساعة التاسعة والساعة العاشرة تقريبا في اليوم المذكور.

The supervisor of the morning shift for the day before yesterday Tuesday 8th March has informed us that you were absent without leave from your duties ('job') in Engineering Department between nine and ten o'clock approximately on the aforementioned day.

3. Numerals in handwriting

In all handwriting (*ruqʿa* or other) the numeral ٢ is usually ۲ ; ٣ is usually ۳ or ۳ . Avoid writing the numeral 2 by hand as ٢, since it can be mistaken for handwritten ٣.

Exercise 1. Read aloud:

e.g.: جاءت جريدة اليوم بصور افتتاح البرلمان الجديد.

jā' at jarīdat al-yawm bi-ṣuwar iftitāḥ al-barlamān al-jadīd.

١ اذا كان ممثلو العمال حاضرين للمفاوضة فإن طرف الإدارة حاضر ايضا.

٢ ان انخفاض الإنتاج في الشرق الأوسط هو ليس السبب الوحيد لارتفاع الأسعار العالمية.

٣ اول نقطة على برنامج الحكومة الاشتراكية الجديدة هي استقرار زيادة صادراتنا الزراعية من اجل تأييد اقتصاد البلاد.

٤ قد فاوضنا مدة طويلة حتى الوصول الي موافقة على تعويض مقبول للعمال.

٥ اننا نرفض تماما شرحهم لعدم دفع هذا الدين لأنهم يعرفون بالضبط شروط قروض البنك.

٦ فيما يتعلق بتوقيع العقد نفضل ان تنتظروا رجوع مدير قسم المحاسبات لأن جدول الاستثمارات المقترح معقد جدا.

٧ تريد الشركة تطبيق شروط دفع مقبولة لجميع زبائنها دون اي تمييز بين الكبار والصغار.

٨ يطلب رئيس الهندسة مساعدتنا لتسوية خلاف حدث في قسمه بين ثلاثة عمال النوبة الليلية ومشرفهم.

٩ اننا نعتبر ان الاقتراح ايجابي ومقبول وننوي ان نطلب موافقة المدير العام خلال الاجتماع المقبل.

١٠ نشكركم على حضوركم في المؤتمر الأخير وخاصة على اقتراحاتكم المفيدة في البحوث المالية.

Exercise 2. Write, using the *ruq'a* forms you have learned:

e.g.: نرجو تأييدكم في هذا الوضع الصعب للشركة.

نرجو تأييدكم في هذا الوضع الصعب للشركة.

١ ما هو رأي وزارة الداخلية في مطالب الولايات المتّحدة؟

٢ ان كلّ مستقبل حزبنا يتوقّف على الانتخابات الإقليمية.

٣ إحدى مشاكلنا في تنمية القطاع الخاصّ في هذا البلاد هي عدم وجود نقل عامّ مناسب للعمّال.

٤ ان الضريبة تبلغ ٢٠٪ تقريبًا من تكاليف إنتاجنا في هذا المصنع.

٥ لو تمكنّا من الرأسمال المناسب لاستطعنا ان نستفيد من هذه الفرصة الاستثمارية الممتازة.

٦ تقدّم المتظاهرون حتّى ميدان البرلمان ولكنهم وقفوا وانسحبوا عندما لقوا الشرطة أمام بناية المجلس.

٧ لا يوجد محلّ للناقلات الكبرى وصار ضروريًا تمديد الميناء كلّه.

٨ ترتفع أسعار المنتجات البترولية على السوق العالمية أسرع ممّا ينخفض مستوى إنتاج النفط الخام في أكثرية الحقول الهامه.

٩ كان بعض الطلأب غائبين عن الاجتماع الافتتاحي للكلّية الهندسية.

١٠ لن تنحلّ مشاكل الشرق الأوسط إلاّ إذا أخذت كلّ الأطراف بعين الاعتبار مصالح الفلسطينيين.

2 Words – 1

- Nouns of activity, person, instrument and place
- Using a dictionary

1. General

Many nouns relating to activities are derived from verb roots. Examples (with variants) are given below. Others are already familiar to you.

2. Activity

For the activity we can use as model طباخة *ṭibākha* 'cookery'; for the person pursuing the activity, the model طبّاخ *ṭabbākh* 'cook':

Root	Activity		Person		
طبخ	طباخة	*ṭibākha*	طبّاخ	*ṭabbākh*	cookery, cook
نجر	نجارة	*nijāra*	نجّار	*najjār*	carpentry, carpenter
نقش	نقاشة	*niqāsha*	نقّاش	*naqqāsh*	painting, painter
خبز	خبازة	*khibāza*	خبّاز	*khabbāz*	bakery, baker
سبك	سباكة	*sibāka*	سبّاك	*sabbāk*	plumbing, plumber
برد	برادة	*birāda*	برّاد	*barrād*	metalwork, -er
خيط	خياطة	*khiyāṭa*	خيّاط	*khayyāṭ*	sewing, tailor
جرح	جراحة	*jirāḥa*	جرّاح	*jarrāḥ*	surgery, surgeon
صرف			صرّاف	*ṣarrāf*	moneychanger
حفر			حفّار	*ḥaffār*	driller
كنس			كنّاس	*kannās*	sweeper
بني	بناء	*binā'* (NB)	بنّاء	*bannā'* (NB)	building, builder
لحم	لحام	*liḥām* (NB)	لحّام	*laḥḥām*	welding, welder; butcher(y)

Note:

- Remember that verbal nouns (B 28) also express an activity:

كتابة I writing طيران I aviation, flying

تبريد وتكييف *tabrīd wa-takyīf* II refrigeration and airconditioning

- Plurals of the persons are sound. Any can be made feminine where appropriate: خيّاطة *khayyāṭa* dressmaker
- Often an active participle (B 26) is used for the person:

تاجر تجّار	I trader	مقرّر	II reporter
محاسب	III accountant	مستورد	X importer

3. Instrument and place

For the instrument used in a task, we have models مفتاح مفاتيح *miftāḥ mafātīḥ* and مطبخ مطابخ *miṭbakh maṭābikh* 'stove':

Root	Instrument		
فتح	مفتاح مفاتيح	*miftāḥ mafātīḥ*	key, switch
سمر	مسمار مسامير	*mismār masāmīr*	nail, rivet
نشر	منشار مناشير	*minshār manāshīr*	saw
قيس	مقياس مقاييس	*miqyās maqāyīs*	gauge, meter
طبخ	مطبخ مطابخ	*miṭbakh maṭābikh*	stove
برد	مبرد مبارد	*mibrad mabārid*	file, rasp
ثقب	مثقب مثاقب	*mithqab mathāqib*	drill, bit
كنس	مكنسة مكانس	*miknasa* (NB) *makānis*	broom
نشف	منشفة مناشف	*minshafa* (NB) *manāshif*	towel

For the place of activity we have models مطبخ مطابخ *maṭbakh maṭābikh* 'kitchen', مصرف مصارف *maṣrif maṣārif* 'bank' and مكتبة مكاتب *maktaba makātib* 'library':

Root	Place		
طبخ	مطبخ مطابخ	*maṭbakh maṭābikh*	kitchen
نزل	منزل منازل	*manzil manāzil*	residence
دخل	مدخل مداخل	*madkhal madākhil*	entrance
خرج	مخرج مخارج	*makhraj makhārij*	exit
فرق	مفرق مفارق	*mafraq mafāriq*	crossroad
لعب	ملعب ملاعب	*mal'ab malā'ib*	stadium, playground
طعم	مطعم مطاعم	*maṭ'am maṭā'im*	restaurant

صرف	مصرف مصارف	*maṣrif maṣārif*	bank
عرض	معرِض معارض	*ma'riḍ ma'āriḍ*	exhibition hall
قهو	مقهًى\المقهى	*maqhan, al-maqha* (weak)	
pl.	مقاه\المقاهي	*maqāhin, al-maqāhī*	coffee-house
كتب	مكتبة مكاتب	*maktaba makātib*	library, bookshop
ملك	مملكة ممالك	*mamlaka mamālik*	kingdom
حطّ	محطّة	*mahaṭṭa* (sound pl.)	stop, station

Note:

- with a few roots, the place form indicates *time*:
  root وعد , noun موعد مواعد *maw'id mawā'id* appointment
- some passive participles (B 26) of Forms VII-X are used also as nouns of place:
  مؤتمر VIII conference مختبر VIII laboratory
  انقلب *inqálaba* VII to be overthrown,
  منقلب *munqálab* place of defeat
  استوصف *istawṣafa* X to consult (a doctor),
  مستوصف *mustawṣaf* clinic
  استشفى *istashfa* X to seek a cure, مستشفًى hospital

4. Using a dictionary

The newest dictionaries (e.g. *Arabic Dictionary*, N. Awde & K. Smith, 2004) list Arabic entries alphabetically by the word. Older dictionaries (e.g. *Dictionary of Modern Written Arabic*, Hans Wehr) list Arabic entries by the *root*; thus معلّم is found under علم . When using a root-based dictionary, remember that ا\ى are not root letters; for example دعا appears under دعو, صارت under صير, and يبقى under بقي .

5. Vocabulary: شؤون الموظّفين *shu'ūn al-muwaẓẓafīn*

Personnel

استخدم *istakhdama* X to recruit, engage

استقال (NB: root قيل) *istaqāla* X to resign
اشتغل *ishtághala* VIII to work
أهلية *'ahlīya* qualification
بدل أبدال *badal 'abdāl* benefit, allowance
تقاعد *taqā'ada* VI to retire
خبرة *khibra* experience
خدمة *khidma* service
خطّط *khaṭṭaṭa* II to plan
خطّة خطط *khiṭṭa khiṭaṭ* plan, scheme
رتبة رتب *rutba rutab* grade, rank
رفع يرفع تقريراً إلى *rafa'a yarfa'u* I *taqrīran 'ila* to report to
شغل إضافي *shughl 'iḍāfī* overtime (work)
صندوق صناديق *ṣandūq ṣanādīq* fund
طوّر *ṭawwara* II to develop
عزل يعزل (عن) *'azala ya'zilu* I *('an)* to dismiss (from)
عزل (عن) *'azl ('an)* dismissal (from)
علاوة *'ilāwa* benefit, allowance
فحص فحوص *faḥṣ fuḥūṣ* examination, inquiry
قوة عاملة *quwa 'āmila* workforce
معاش (تقاعد) *ma'āsh (taqā'ud)* (retirement) pension
مقابل *muqābil* remuneration
مقابلة *muqābala* interview
ممرّض\ممرّضة *mumarriḍ(a)* nurse
مندوب\ممثّل (نقابة) عمّال *mandūb/mumaththil (niqābat) 'ummāl* shop steward
مهنة مهن *mihna mihan* (also:) career
مؤهّل *mu'ahhil* qualification; *mu'ahhal* qualified, skilled
نظام أنظمة *niẓām 'anẓima* regulation, rule
نقابة عمّال *niqābat 'ummāl* trade union

Exercise 1. Form nouns of activity and person from the root shown:

e.g.: *nijāra, najjār* نجر ← نجارة، نجّار

١ خبز　　٢ لحم　　٣ بني　　٤ برد

٥ طبخ　　٦ خيط　　٧ جرح　　٨ نقش

and the places of activity from the root shown:

e.g.: *majlis majālis* جلس ← مجلس مجالس

١ طير　　٢ لعب　　٣ كتب　　٤ طعم

٥ حطّ　　٦ درس　　٧ خرج　　٨ صنع

Exercise 2. Study this organisation chart and answer the questions:

موجز جدول تنظيم شركة المواصلات الحديثة

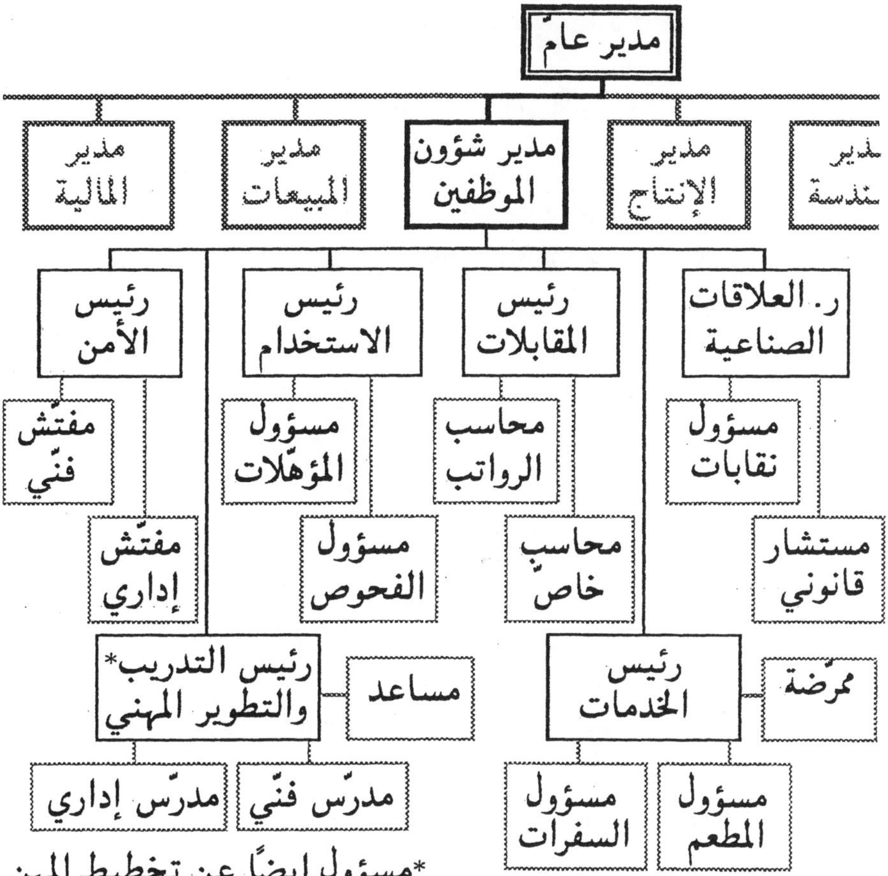

*مسؤول إيضًا عن تخطيط المهن

NB: On a chart the job titles are nominally masc. except for designated female posts. A woman appointee sometimes uses a feminine title.

١ كم مديراً ترى (كاملاً أو جزئيًا) على هذا الجدول؟ اذكر مسؤولياتهم.
٢ من مسؤول عن أمن البنايات والماكينات؟ لمن يرفع تقريراً؟
٣ أحد هؤلاء الموظفين محام. من هو؟
٤ يرفع كم رئيساً تقريراً لمدير شؤون الموظفين؟
٥ لو كان إضراب عند اللحّامين أو النقّاشين مثلاً، لكانت لمن مسؤولية المفاوضة مع المضربين؟
٦ لمن يرفع تقريراً رئيس الخدمات؟
٧ لرئيس التدريب والتطوير المهني أيّة مسؤولية إضافية؟
٨ ما هو الفرق بين مدير ورئيس ومسؤول حسب هذا الجدول؟
٩ كم رتبة أو مستوى استخدام توجد على الجدول؟
١٠ في رأيك، ما هي مسؤوليات المحاسب الخاصّ (انظر تحت رئيس المقابلات)؟

Exercise 3. Complete the sentence with nouns of activity, person, instrument or place as appropriate:

e.g.: نعمل التجارب في ... الكلّية. ← ... في مختبر الكلّية.

١ يحفر الـ.. البئر بواسطة ... .
٢ يحضّر الـ.. الأكل في الـ.. و يأكله الضيوف في الـ... .
٣ يقف القطار في كلّ الـ..ات بين العاصمة والساحل.
٤ يجتمع البرلمان عادةً في الـ.. الوطني.
٥ لقسم إنتاج الـ.. ثلاثة ... لصنعها.
٦ في هذا الـ.. ...ون متخصّصون في كلّ نوع من الجراحة.

Exercise 4. Under what entry in a root-based dictionary do we find:

e.g.: جرى ← جري

١ اتّصال	٢ يقفون	٣ نصطنعه	٤ تنسون
٥ اتّخاذ	٦ قلنا	٧ استفاد	٨ اكتشاف

3 Words – 2

- Irregular nouns أب *'ab*, أخ *'akh*
- Masculine proper names

1. أب *'ab*, أخ *'akh*

The nouns أب آباء *'ab 'ābā'* 'father' and أخ إخوة *'akh 'ikhwa* 'brother' are irregular in the singular when carrying a possessive suffix other than ي..., or when used as the theme of a construct. In these situations they follow the m. sing. pattern of ذو (B 24), i.e. nominative أبو\أخو, accusative أبا\أخا, and genitive أبي\أخي. Examine:

possessive other than ي...:

أبوه مختار القرية. *'abūhu mukhtār al-qáriya.*
His father is mayor of the village.

هل تعرف أخاها؟ *('akhāha)* Do you know her brother?

هذا هو بيت أبيهم. *(bayt 'abīhim)* This is their father's house.

theme of construct:

جاء أبو أحمد. *jā' 'abū 'aḥmad.* Ahmad's father came.

هنا أبو المختار. *('abu l-mukhtār)*
Here is the mayor's father.

يعرف أخا صديقي. *('akhā ṣadīqī)*
He knows my friend's brother.

لأبي الطالب *li-'abi ṭ-ṭālib* for the student's father

Remember that a final long vowel is often pronounced short (B 1).

In all other situations (including when suffixed with ي... 'my', and in the plural) these nouns are regular:

قد ساعدوا أبي كثيراً. *qad sā'adū 'abī kathīran.*
They have helped my father greatly.

يسكن إخوة زوجها في مصر. *yaskun 'ikhwat zawjiha fī miṣr.*
Her husband's brothers live in Egypt.

Note also:

- أخت أخوات *'ukht 'akhawāt* 'sister', regular.
- أب expresses also 'Father' for a Christian cleric:

  الأب\أبونا يوسف *al-'ab/'abūna yūsuf* Father Joseph
- أخ is also used for a close colleague or friend:

  حضر أخونا\الأخ رشيد. *ḥaḍar 'akhūna/al-'akh rashīd.*

  Our friend/colleague Rashid attended.
- the dual forms أبوان\...ين *'abawān/-ayn* and أخوان\...ين *'akhawān/-ayn.*
- the plural إخوان *'ikhwān* 'brethren' (of an association):

  الإخوان المسلمون *al-'ikhwān al-muslimūn*

  the Muslim Brotherhood ('Brethren')

2. Masculine proper names

Proper names are definite in meaning. But masculine personal names not resembling a *verb tense* and not ending ...ان *-ān*, have *indefinite* case-endings; for our purposes this means that in the accusative the name adds the indefinite ending ...اً *-an*:

رأينا محمّداً وتوفيقاً وجميلاً. *(muḥammadan wa-tawfīqan wa-jamīlan)* We saw Muhammad, Tawfiq and Jamil.

But: نعرف أحمد وعثمان. *('aḥmad wa-'uthmān)*

We know Ahmad and Othman.

3. Vocabulary: المجتمع *al-mujtáma'* The Community

اجتماع *ijtimā'* (also:) society

اجتماعي *ijtimā'ī* social

أرمل أرامل *'armal 'arāmil* widower

أرملة أرامل *'armala 'arāmil* widow

أعان (في) *'a'āna* IV *(fī* thing*)* to subsidise

إمرأة (المرأة) نسوان *'imra'a (al-mar'a) niswān* woman

بلدية	*baladīya* (also:) town council
تزوّج (من\ب\على)	*tazawwaja* V *(min/bi-/ʿala)* to get married (to)
جمعية	*jamʿīya* association
خدمات اجتماعية	*khidmāt ijtimāʿīya* social services
دخل	*dakhl* income
رجل رجال	*rajul rijāl* man
رخّص (ل ب)	*rakhkhaṣa* II *(li-* person, *bi-* thing*)* to license, to permit
رخصة رخص	*rukhṣa rukhaṣ* licence, permit
روضة رياض (أطفال)	*rawḍa riyāḍ (ʾaṭfāl)* kindergarten
رئيس بلدية	*raʾīs baladīya* mayor
زواج	*ziwāj* marriage
زوج أزواج	*zawj ʾazwāj* husband
زوجة	*zawja* wife
ساكن سكّان	*sākin sukkān* inhabitant
سجّل	*sajjala* II to register
سكن	*sakan* housing
شيخ شيوخ	*shaykh shuyūkh* elder, senator
ضمان اجتماعي	*ḍamān ijtimāʿī* social security
عرس أعراس	*ʿurs ʾaʿrās* wedding
فقير فقراء	*faqīr fuqarāʾ* poor
متزوّج (من\ب\على)	*mutazawwij (min/bi-/ʿala)* married (to)
مختار مخاتير	*mukhtār makhātīr* mayor (of a village)
مركز جماعي	*markaz jamāʿī* community centre
مستحقّ (ل)	*mustaḥiqq (li-)* deserving (of), eligible (for)
مسلم	*muslim* Muslim
مسيحي	*masīḥī* Christian
منح يمنح	*manaḥa yamnaḥu* I to grant to
منح	*manḥ* granting, award
ناد\النادي أندية	*nādin, an-nādī* (weak) *ʾándiya* club

يهودي يهود *yahūdī yahūd* Jew(ish)

Exercise 1. Complete, with the correct form of أب\أخ in the singular:

e.g.: ... *'akhā zamīlina?* هل تعرف (أخ) زميلنا ؟ ← ...أخا زميلنا ؟

١ هل تعرف الـ(أخ) ؟ ٢ تقاعد (أب)ه قبل سنتين.

٣ (أخ)ي مختار لثالث مرّة. ٤ كان (أخ)ه طالبًا.

٥ درسوا عند (أب) الأستاذ الحالي ٦ أين يسكن الـ(أب) ؟

٧ أفعال الأطفال مسؤولية (أب)هم. ٨ يعمل في قسم (أخ)ك.

٩ في وقت (أب)كم كان أسهل. ١٠ طلب مساعدة (أخ)ه.

Exercise 2. Under what entry in a root-based dictionary do we find:

e.g.: مربّاة ← ربي

١ صرنا ٢ أخيراً ٣ متزوّج ٤ مضاف

٥ متظاهرين ٦ ابتداءً ٧ استثنائي ٨ ألماني

٩ اتّفاقية ١٠ اتّخذوا ١١ اجتماعية ١٢ إرسال

Exercise 3. Give the word answering to the definition:

e.g.: جماعة اشخاص مسؤولين عن ادارة بلد ← بلدية

١ من يعمل ملابس للرجال ٢ محل لتحضير الأكل

٣ محلّ يظل اطفال صغار ويلعبون فيه

٤ اسلوب رسمي لمساعدة الناس وخاصة الفقراء

٥ مكان يشرب الناس القهوة فيه ٦ ساكن القرية الرئيسي

٧ مدينة قديمة تهم المسلمين والمسيحيين واليهود

٨ بناية عامة يجتمع فيها سكان القرية في الوقت الفاضي

٩ رجل متزوج: امرأة متزوجة ١٠ مصدر الفعل 'سجّل'

١١ هذه الطفلة هي بنتي وأنا ......ها.

١٢ رجال اعضاء جمعية ذات مصالح او اغراض خاصة (إخو ......)

4 Words – 3

- Compound adjectives and nouns

1. General

We have already studied some compound adjectives and nouns, such as expressions with ذو (B 35) and negative expressions formed with غير (B 23) and عدم (B 28). Here we examine other compounds.

2. Compound adjectives: عديم *'adīm*, قابل *qābil*

عديم *'adīm* **etc.** The adjectival equivalent of عدم, using the same structure, is عديم *'adīm* 'lacking (in)', which produces a negative construct, the opposite of ذو (etc., B. 24):

عدم الاهتمام lack of attention, inattention

عديم (الـ)اهتمام *'adīm (al-)ihtimām*
lacking attention, inattentive

عديم الثقافة *'adīm ath-thaqāfa* lacking culture, uncultured (= غير مثقّف *ghayr muthaqqaf*)

عديم + verbal noun can give the same meaning as غير + adjective or participle. Remember to define explicitly only the *attribute* of the construct, not the theme, to make the expression definite. Examine the following possible compounds:

- **affirmative** with ذو (etc.) or with adjective/participle:

زميل ذو اهلية\زميل مؤهّل a qualified colleague

زميل ذو أهلية مناسبة a colleague with an appropriate qualification

الزميل ذو الأهلية\الزميل المؤهّل the qualified colleague

الزميل ذو الأهلية المناسبة the appropriately qualified colleague

(الـ)مساهم ذو (الـ)أموال (الـ)كافية *((al-)musāhim)* a/the shareholder with sufficient funds

- **negative** with عديم or غير:

زميل عديم أهلية\ غير مؤهّل an unqualified colleague

الزميل عديم الأهلية\الزميل غير المؤهّل the unqualified colleague

زميل عديم أهلية مناسبة\ الأهلية المناسبة a colleague without an appropriate/ the appropriate qualification

الزميل عديم الأهلية المناسبة the colleague without the appropriate qualification

(الـ)مساهم عديم (الـ)أموال (الـ)كافية *((al-)musāhim)* a/the shareholder without sufficient funds

You may encounter the article incorrectly added to عديم\غير .

قابـل ل *qābil li-*. The active participial expression قابل ل *qābil li-* 'susceptible to' + definite verbal noun can express the equivalent of English '-able', '-ible':

فكرة\أفكار قابلة للاهتمام a remarkable idea/remarkable ideas

When this compound is made definite, قابل itself also has the article, since the expression is not a construct but is prepositional with ل:

هذه الفكرة القابلة للاهتمام this remarkable idea

الطاقة القابلة للتجديد ('the') renewable energy

The compound is negated as usual with غير:

اقتراح غير قابل للشرح an inexplicable proposal

هذا الاقتراح غير القابل للشرح this inexplicable proposal

Contrast this last expression with the following, which is an equation:

هذا الاقتراح غير قابل للشرح. This proposal is inexplicable.

لا... *lā-*. A few relative adjectives have a negative form with لا... *lā-*:

إنساني\لاإنساني *(lā-)'insānī* (in)human, (in)humane

لاسلكي *lā-silkī* wireless

from which also abstract nouns (B 10) have been derived:

اللاإنسانية *al-lā-'insānīya* inhumanity

اللامركزية *al-lā-markazīya* decentralisation

Use only known words of this pattern; do not form your own.

3. Doubled adjectives

Doubled adjectives are easier in Arabic than in English. Both adjectives keep their full Arabic form, including agreement:

التعاون العربي(-)الأوروبي Euro-Arab cooperation
(the hyphen is optional in the Arabic)
النظرية الاجتماعية الاقتصادية socio-economic theory
النزاع العربي الإسرائيلي the Arab-Israeli conflict
خلاف شمالي جنوبي a north-south dispute

4. Compound adjectives and nouns: شبه *shibh*, نصف *niṣf*

The noun شبه أشباه *shibh 'ashbāh* 'resemblance', when used in construct with an adjective, gives the meaning 'semi-', 'quasi-' etc.:

مراسلة شبه رسمية *murāsala shibh rasmīya*
semi-official/quasi-official correspondence
بصورة شبه رسمية semi/quasi-officially
العمّال شبه المؤهّلون the semi-skilled labour ('workers')

The device is also used to make a few compound nouns:

شبه جزيرة *shibh jazīra* peninsula
(pl. أشباه جزر *'ashbāh juzur*; جزيرة جزر *jazīra juzur* island)
شبة الجزيرة العربية *shibh al-jazīra l-'arabīya*
the Arabian Peninsula
شبه القارّة الهندية *shibh al-qārra l-hindīya*
the Indian Subcontinent

The noun نصف أنصاف *niṣf 'anṣāf* 'half' in construct makes some compound adjectives:

نصف سنوي semi-annually, bi-annually
منطقة نصف مستقلّة a semi-autonomous ('-independent') region

5. Compound nouns: كبار *kibār*, صغار *ṣighār*

In B 2 we had the adjectives كبير and صغير in the meanings 'senior' and 'junior' respectively: موظّف كبير\صغير . Their plural forms are also used in definite construct with certain plural nouns to give the same meanings. The construct is always definite, the definiteness or indefiniteness in connotation being inferred from the context:

كبار المسؤولين\المأمورين (the) senior officials
لصغار ضبّاطهم (*ḍubbāṭihim*) for their junior officers
مع كبار أعضاء الحزب with (the) senior party members

The attribute may also indicate a group, which can then be singular:

كبار الجمعية senior (members) of the association

مختلف can also be used in this manner, with indefinite meaning:

بمختلف الأسباب for various reasons

6. Vocabulary: الإدارة *al-'idāra* Management

أدار *'adāra* IV to manage
استغرق *istaghraqa* X to last
اعتمد على *i'támada* VIII *'ala* to rely on
أمّم *'ammama* II to nationalise
أموال *'amwāl* (also, in pl.:) funds, resources
انعقد *in'áqada* VII to be convened
بيانات *bayānāt* (inan. pl., also:) details, particulars
تشجيع (على) *tashjī' ('ala)* incentive, encouragement (to)
جدول أعمال *jadwal 'a'māl* agenda
جهد جهود *juhd juhūd* effort
حد يحد *ḥadda yaḥuddu* I to limit
حوّل *ḥawwala* II to transfer
خسر يخسر *khasira yakhsaru* I to lose
خسارة *khasāra* loss
دافع دوافع *dāfi' dawāfi'* motivation

دائرة دوائر *dā'ira dawā'ir* directorate
دائم *dā'im* permanent
دور أدوار *dawr 'adwār* rôle
دورة *dawra* round (of talks etc.)
ربح يربح *rabiḥa yarbaḥu* I to profit
ربح أرباح *ribḥ 'arbāḥ* profit
سلك أسلاك *silk 'aslāk* wire
سهم أسهم *sahm 'as-hum* share (of stock)
شارك (في) *shāraka* III (*fī*) to participate (in)
شريك شركاء *sharīk shurakā'* partner, associate
شغّل *shaghghala* II to operate
صاحب (أصحاب) عمل *ṣāḥib* (pl. *'aṣḥāb*) *'amal* employer
ضابط ضبّاط *ḍābiṭ ḍubbāṭ* officer
ظرف ظروف *ẓarf ẓurūf* circumstance
عادي *'ādī* ordinary
غير عادي *ghayr 'ādī* extraordinary
فائدة فوائد *fā'ida fawā'id* (monetary) interest
قدّر *qaddara* II to estimate
مال *māl* (also, in sing.:) wealth
مجلس إدارة *majlis 'idāra* board of directors
محدود *maḥdūd* limited, Ltd.
مساهم *musāhim* shareholder
مؤقّت *mu'aqqat* temporary
ناطق\ناطقة بلسان *nāṭiq(a) bi-lisān* spokesman (-woman)
نظّم *naẓẓama* II to organise
هيئة *hay'a* group, body
هيكل هياكل *haykal hayākil* structure, framework

Exercise 1. Make definite expressions indefinite and vice versa, where possible:

e.g.: اقتراح غير مقبول ← الاقتراح غير المقبول

١ الأرباح نصف السنوية ٢ الجمعية ذات المال الكثير
٣ معطيات غير محضّرة ٤ اجتماع شبه رسمي
٥ بالأسهم غير العادية ٦ كبار مجلس الإدارة
٧ مواصلات لاسلكية ٨ الفائدة القابلة للدفع فوراً
٩ لمختلف مساهمينا ١٠ هيكل عديم أساس قانوني
١١ في ظروف غير مقبولة لنا ١٢ ترجمة عربية فرنساوية

Exercise 2. Recast, using a relative clause (B 35):

e.g.: مجلس إدارة ذات قوات محدودة
← مجلس إدارة لها\عندها قوات محدودة
majlis 'idāra laha/'indaha quwāt maḥdūda

١ الضرائب القابلة للتقدير بالضبط ٢ فوائد مدفوعة سنويًا
٣ مساهم عديم فهم السوق ٤ أسهمي المشتراة قبل سنة
٥ أرباح غير مقدّرة وغير مشروحة في جريدة اليوم

Exercise 3. Read the passage and answer the questions:

يعقد مجلس اتّحاد إدارات موانئ(1) شمال أفريقيا دورته الواحدة والثلاثين بطرابلس(2) (ليبيا) خلال الفترة(3) ما بين ١٥ و١٧ فبراير الجاري لدراسة برنامج عمل الاتّحاد لسنة ٢٠٠٥ ...

....

وسيشارك في أشغال هذه الدورة الرؤساء والمدراء العامّون للهيئات المينائية بدول الاتّحاد وهي موريتانيا والمغرب والجزائر وتونس والجماهيرية(4) الليبية ومصر والسودان.

(from العرب *Al-Arab* newspaper, 9.2.05)

(1) موانئ *mawānī'* ports (alternative pl. of ميناء)
(2) طرابلس *ṭarābulus* Tripoli (3) فترة فترات *fatra fatarāt* period
(4) جماهيرية *jamāhīrīya* Jamahiriya ('State of the Masses')

١ ما هي دول أعضاء الاتّحاد؟ ٢ من شارك في المؤتمر؟
٣ ما كان أهمّ موضوع البحوث؟ ٤ كم يومًا استغرق المؤتمر؟
٥ اذكر أربعة موان هامّة في شمال أفريقيا.

5 Words – 4

- Dual and feminine plural pronouns, possessive adjectives and verbs

1. General

The dual and the feminine plural exist only in the 2nd and 3rd persons. Noun, adjective and demonstrative forms are covered in B 3 and 4.
The Appendix ('B App'), paragraphs 2 to 5 (Tables 7 to 10) of the *Basic Arabic Workbook* gives the pronoun, possessive, relative and verb forms. Here we explore the use of these forms.
Dual forms are the same for animate or inanimate. Feminine plural forms are only animate, and refer only to all-female groups. Further, there is no shortened pronunciation for the feminine plural endings. Beyond these provisions, all the rules we have studied for suffixing and for sentence structure apply equally to the dual and the feminine plural.

2. Dual subject pronouns and suffixes

See B 5, 12, 15 and App, Table 7. Dual subject pronouns and dual suffixes do not vary for gender. They are formed by adding ا... *-a* to the appropriate *(masculine) animate plural* form:

هل أنتما طالبان\طالبتان؟ *('antuma)* Are you (two) students?

إذا كان عندكما عمل *('indakuma)* if you both have work

رأيناهما. *ra'aynāhuma.* We saw both of them (people/things).

اتّصلنا بهما. *(bihima)* We contacted them both.

Remember that in an English plural there may lurk a dual:

عنده التقديران. هل قارنهما؟ *(qāranahuma)*

He has the two estimates. Has he compared them (= both)?

اشتغل الأخوان كلّ اليوم في مطعمهما. *(ishtághal al-'akhawān ... fī maṭ'amihima)* The two brothers worked all day in their restaurant.

3. Dual verbs

See B 11, 14, 17, 25 and App, paragraphs 3-5 and Tables 9, 10.

B App, Tables 9 and 10 show the dual verb endings for past and present. B App, paragraph 5 shows the dual subjunctive, jussive and imperative. Note:

- The 2nd-person forms do not vary for gender; the 3rd-person forms do.
- Care is needed with the final-weak verbs.
- The dual ending ا..., however pronounced without a suffix, becomes *-ā́-* (long and stressed) when an object suffix is added.

جلس الزميلان وشربا قهوتهما. *(wa-sharaba qahwatahuma)*
The (two) colleagues sat and drank their coffee.

إنّ الطرفين لا يستطيعان أن يتّفقا على التفاصيل. *(lā yastaṭī'ān 'an yattáfiqā)* The two parties cannot agree on the details.

قرآ العقد ووقّعاه. *qara'a l-'aqd wa-waqqa'āhu.*
They (both) read the contract and signed it.

اجلسا. *ijlisā.* Sit down (both of you).

4. Dual relative pronouns

See B 35 and App, Table 8. The dual relative pronoun varies for gender and (unlike the singular and plural) for case. Note also the spelling. For the rest, all the rules for relative clauses apply:

المقرّران اللذان كتبا المقالة *(alladhān kataba)*
the two reporters who wrote the article

المنتجان الرئيسيان اللذين يبيعونهما *(alladhayn yabī'ūnahuma)*
the two chief products which they selll

النقطتان اللتين تركّزوا فيهما *an-nuqṭatān allatayn tarakkazū fīhima* the two points they concentrated on

نقطتان ركّزوا فيهما *nuqṭatān rakkazū fīhima* (indefinite antecedent, no relative pronoun) two points they concentrated on

5. Feminine plural subject pronouns and suffixes

See B 5, 12, 15 and App, Table 7. For subject pronouns and for suffixes the feminine plural is formed by substituting ...نَّ *-nna* for the final ...ـم *-m* of the appropriate *(masculine) animate plural* form:

هل أنتنّ طالبات؟ *('antunna)* Are you students?
إذا كان عندكنّ عمل *('indakunna)* if you have work
رأيناهنّ. *ra'aynāhunna*. We saw them.
اتّصلنا بهنّ. *(bihinna)* We contacted them.

6. Feminine plural verbs

See B 11, 14, 17, 25 and App, paragraphs 3-5 and Tables 9, 10.

B App, Tables 9 and 10 show the feminine plural verb endings for past and present. B App paragraph 5 shows the feminine plural subjunctive, jussive and imperative. Note:

- As with pronouns and suffixes, the verb forms are best derived from the corresponding *(masculine) animate plural*; replace ...تم *-tum* with ...تنّ *-tunna* and ...ون\وا *-ūna/-ū* with ...ن *-na*.
- Care is needed with the doubled, hollow and final-weak verbs.
- The unwritten final short vowel *-a* remains short and unstressed when an object suffix is added.

جلست المديرات وشربن قهوتهنّ. *(wa-sharabna qahwatahunna)*
The directors sat and drank their coffee.

إنّ المعلّمات لا يستطعن أن يتّفقن على الجدول. *(lā yastaṭi'na 'an yattafiqna)* The teachers cannot agree on the timetable.

قرأن العقد ووقّعنه. *qará'na l-'aqd wa-waqqá'nahu.*
They read the contract and signed it.

اجلسن. *(ijlisna)* Sit down.

7. Feminine plural relative pronoun

See B 35 and App, Table 8. The feminine plural relative pronoun is invariable. Note also the spelling. The rules for relative clauses apply:

الصحفيات اللواتي كتبن المقالة *(allawāti katabna)* the newswomen who wrote the article

الطبيبات اللواتي نعرفهنّ كلّنا *(allawāti na'rifuhunna kulluna)* the doctors whom we all know

طبيبات نعتمد عليهنّ *('alayhinna)* doctors we rely on

8. Vocabulary: الأكل والشراب *al-'akl wa-sh-sharāb* Food and drink

See also B 10, paragraph 1.

أرزّ *'aruzz* rice
بارد *bārid* cold
برّادة *barrāda* refrigerator
بوزة *būza* ice, ice cream
بيرة *bīra* beer
تناول *tanāwala* III to take (food, drink)
جبنة *jubna* cheese
جوعان جوعى جياع *jaw'ān,* f. *jaw'a,* pl. *jiyā'* hungry
حلو *ḥalw* sweet
حلويات *ḥalwayāt* sweets, dessert
خبز أخباز *khubz 'akhbāz* bread
خضر *khuḍar* vegetables
خلط يخلط *khalaṭa yakhliṭu* I to mix
خمر خمور *khamr khumūr* (m./f.) wine
زبدة *zubda* butter
سخن *sukhn* hot
سكّر *sukkar* sugar
سكّين سكاكين *sikkīn sakākīn* (m./f.) knife
سلاطة *salāṭa* salad
شراب أشربة *sharāb 'ashriba* drink

شوربة *shōrba* soup
شوكة *shawka* fork
صحن صحون *ṣaḥn suḥūn* plate
طبخ يطبخ *ṭabakha yaṭbukhu* I to cook
طحين *ṭaḥīn* flour
عشاء أعشية *'ashā' 'á'shiya* dinner, supper
عصير *'aṣīr* juice
عطشان عطشى عطاش *'aṭshān*, f. *'aṭsha*, pl. *'iṭāsh* thirsty
غداء أغدية *ghadā' 'ághdiya* lunch
غذاء أغذية *ghidhā' 'ághdhiya* food(stuff)
فاكهة فواكه *fākiha fawākih* fruit
فطور *faṭūr* breakfast
فنجان فناجين *finjān fanājīn* cup
كاس كؤوس *kās ku'ūs* a glass
لبن *laban* milk
لحم لحام *laḥm liḥām* meat
ماء مياه *mā'* water
ماء معدني *mā' ma'dinī* mineral water
مشروب *mashrūb* drink
ملح أملاح *milḥ 'amlāḥ* (m./f.) salt
ملعقة ملاعق *mil'aqa malā'iq* spoon

Exercise 1. Make dual the underlined words and suffixes:

e.g.: *'akala faṭūrahuma.* أكل فطوره. ← أكلا فطورهما.

١ أكلت عشاءها.
٢ شربت قهوتها وخرجت.
٣ يأكلن دائمًا في المطعم.
٤ لا تأكل البنات في المدرسة.
٥ هل حضّرتم الشوربة؟
٦ وصلت رسالات إليكم.
٧ وصلت رسالاتكم.
٨ ضع الصحون على الطاولة.
٩ خذيها من هناك.
١٠ وصل لتناول غداءه.

Why are تأكل (no. 4) and وصلت (6, 7) not made dual too?

Exercise 2. Make feminine plural:

e.g.: *yaṭbukhna al-ghadā'*. يطبخن الغداء. ← يطبخون الغداء.

١ إنّ البنت تذهب ألى مدرستها. ٢ تذهب البنت ألى مدرستها.
٣ خذي تفاحتك معك. ٤ أكلوا فطورهم في البستان.
٥ كانوا يلعبون مع أخوته. ٦ لا تنسوا أن تأمروا الفواكه.

Exercise 3. Make the dual and feminine plural expressions (a) masculine singular, (b) feminine singular, (c) masculine plural:

e.g.: *'akal, 'akalat, 'akalū* أكلوا، أكلت، أكل ← أكلن

١ شربا شايهما. ٢ اذكرا اسمكما على الورقة.
٣ صحفيات ذوات خبرة ممتازة ٤ كيف جاويتا على طلبكنّ؟
٥ سافرن إلى مصر ليزرن صديقاتهنّ. ٦ لم يقولا إلاّ الحقّ.

Exercise 4. Read this report and then retell it in your own words:

قال وزير التجارة العراقي محمّد الجبوري *(al-jabūrī)* أمس أنّ بلاده بدأت في إعلان مناقصة(1) عامّة لشراء(2) الأغذية في خطوة قد(3) تنهي(4) سنوات من السرّية(5) والفساد(6) في قطاع قيمته(7) ميليارات(8) الدولارات.

وقال الجبوري أنّ الوزارة نشرت بالفعل مناقصةً لشراء ١٠٠ ألف طنّ من طحين "دقيق"(9) القمح(10) في الصحف وفي موقعها(11) على الإنترنت وستنشر قريباً مناقصةً أخرى لشراء ١٠٠ ألف طنّ من الأرزّ وأضاف "إنّنا نفتح الباب أمام الجميع لن تكون هناك أيّ محاباة(12). كلّ شيء سيكون على الإنترنت".

(from الحياة *Al-Hayat* newspaper, 22.7.2004)

(1) مناقصة *munāqaṣa* call for tenders (2) شراء *shirā'* purchase
(3) قد (+ *present tense*) perhaps (4) أنهى *'anha* IV to bring to an end
(5) سرّية *sirrīya* secrecy (6) فساد *fasād* corruption
(7) قيمة قيم *qīma qíyam* value (8) ميليار *mīliyār* milliard (10^9)
(9) دقيق دقاق *daqīq diqāq* fine (10) قمح قموح *qamaḥ qumūḥ* wheat
(11) موقع مواقع *mawqi' mawāqi'* site (12) محاباة *muḥābā* favouritism

6 Words – 5

- Passive

1. General

With a verb in the *active* voice (المعلوم *al-ma'lūm*) the subject performs the action or experiences the situation:

كتب\يكتب الطبيب التقرير. *katab/yaktub aṭ-ṭabīb at-taqrīr.*

All the tenses we have used so far are active.

With a verb in the *passive* voice (المجهول *al-majhūl*) the subject *undergoes* or *suffers* the action of the verb:

كتب\يكتب التقرير. *kutib/yuktab at-taqrīr.*

The report was/is (being) written.

Here the grammatical subject is التقرير ; it does not perform the action but undergoes it. We have met the passive concept in two instances:

- Form VII verbs (B 22), active but many with passive meaning:

  انحلّت\تنحلّ المشكلة. *inḥallat/tanḥall al-mushkila.*

  The problem was/is solved.

- the passive participle (B 27):

  مشكلة محلولة a resolved problem

The Arabic passive tenses differ from the active tenses only in the vowels of the prefixes and of the verb root. The passive vowel pattern is regular throughout all classes of verb, in Forms I to X. The personal endings and all the consonants are the same as those of the active.

We need to learn only the past and present tenses, and of these only the third persons (هو, هي, هما, هم, هنّ). The other tenses and persons are too rarely used to concern us.

The rules for short pronunciation and sentence structure apply equally to passive verbs. The rules for agreement also apply, but with some variations examined in paragraph 3 below.

Passive verbs are often avoided and replaced by other structures; some of these are explored in Chapter 12.

The passive has no imperative and no verbal noun.

2. Passive past and present tenses

To make the passive past or present tense, take the corresponding active tense and vowel it as follows (the pattern shown is for هو\هي):

Past tense:	V/VI prefix	VIII/X vowel	Root vowels		Personal ending
Short vowels in root	*tu-*	*u-*	*-u-*	*-i-*	*-a*/*-at*
Long vowels in root	*tu-*	*u-*	*-ū-*	*-ī-*	*-a*/*-at*

Present tense:	Personal prefix	V/VI prefix	Root vowels		Personal ending
Short vowels in root	*yu-*/*tu-*	*-ta-*	*-a-*	*-a-*	*-u*
Long vowels in root	*yū-*/*tū-*	*-ta-*	*-ā-*	*-ā-*	*-u*

For the past tense, note:

- The vowel of Form V and VI prefixes, and the initial weak vowel of Forms VIII and X, are all *u*.
- The 'root vowels' (i.e. those found in the passive form of the root) are *-u-* and *-i-*: this means *-u-* for a root of one syllable, *-u-i-* for a root of two syllables. Form IV past counts as two syllables. This is the pattern for roots ending in a consonant. For roots ending in a vowel, the last *-i-* becomes *-ī* in short pronunciation and *-iya* in full pronunciation for هو, and becomes *-iyat* for هي. Where a root vowel is long in the active form, its replacement vowel is also long in the passive form.
- Add feminine, dual and plural personal endings as usual. They are the same as for the active voice.

For the present tense, note:

- The personal prefix (including the initial vowel of Forms IV, VII,

VIII and X) is *yu-* or *tu-* (*yū/tū* in Form IV of initial-*wāw* verbs).

- The prefixes of Forms V/VI remain *ta-*.
- The root vowels are *-a-* throughout the root.

  This is the pattern for roots ending in a consonant. For roots ending in a vowel, the last *-a* incorporates both final root letter and vowel of the personal ending in both forms of pronunciation. Where a personal prefix vowel or a root vowel is long in the active form, its replacement vowel is also long in the passive.
- Add feminine, dual and plural personal endings as usual.

This is the theory. In practice it is easier to imitate patterns, e.g. (for هو):

past		present		'he/it was/is...'
Root is **one syllable** in length:				
		يكتب	*yuktabu* I	written
		يؤمر	*yu'maru* I	ordered
دلّ	*dulla*	يدلّ	*yudallu* I	shown
قيل	*qīla*	يقال	*yuqālu* I	said
		يرسل	*yursalu* IV	sent
		يوجب	*yūjabu* IV	imposed
		يعطي	*yu'ṭa* IV	given
احتلّ	*uḥtulla*	يحتلّ	*yuḥtallu* VIII	occupied
Root is **two syllables** in length:				
كتب	*kutiba* I			written
قرئ	*quri'a* I			read
نفي	*nūfi/-iya*	ينفي	*yunfa* I	denied
أكّد	*'ukkida*	يؤكّد	*yu'akkadu* II	confirmed
موّل	*muwwila*	يموّل	*yumawwalu* II	financed
ربي	*rubbī/-iya*	يربى	*yurabba* II	brought up
حوول	*ḥūwila* (NB وو)	يحاول	*yuḥāwalu* III	attempted
أرسل	*'ursila** IV			sent
أوجب	*'ūjiba** IV			imposed

أعطي	*'u'ṭīl-iya** IV			given

(* count Form IV as two syllables in the past, see above)

اقترح	*uqtúriḥa*	يقترح	*yuqtáraḥu* VIII	proposed
استعمل	*ustu'mila*	يستعمل	*yusta'malu* X	used
وجد	*wujida*	يوجد	*yūjadu** I	found
وضع	*wuḍi'a*	يوضع	*yūḍa'u** I	put

(* initial root letter و , dropped in the active present, is restored in the passive present and combined with the present prefix. For the form وجد *wujid* see also B 37; for the form يوجد *yūjad* see also B 11, 23)

ووفق	*wūfiq* (NB وو)	يوافق	*yuwāfaq* III	agreed
تنبئ	*tunubbi'a*	يتنبأ	*yutanabba'u* V	forecast
تنوول	*tunūwila*	يتناول	*yutanāwalu* VI	taken (food)
تلقّي	*tuluqqīl-iya*	يتلقّى	*yutalaqqa* V	received
اشتري	*ushtúrīl-iya*	يشترى	*yushtára* VIII	bought
استثني	*ustuthnīl-iya*	يستثنى	*yustathna* X	excepted

The passive is common in newspaper Arabic. Care has to be taken to read the vowels correctly; even television and radio newsreaders make mistakes. Sometimes a significant first vowel ...ُ *u* is pointed in the text:

عُلم أمس أنّ ... *'ulim 'ams 'anna ...*
It was learned yesterday that ...

لا تُبحث اليوم مشاكل طبّية. *lā tubḥath al-yawm mashākil ṭibbīya.*
Medical problems are not being discussed today.

أُكّد من مصادر رسمية ... *'ukkid min maṣādir rasmīya ...*
It was confirmed from official sources ...

3. Instrument, agent, agreement

All the provisions given in B 27 relating to the instrument and to agreement apply equally to passive tenses; but see below for the *agent*:

Instrument; as for the participle:

لم يموّل المستشفى بنقود عامّة. *lam yumawwal al-mustashfa*

bi-nuqūd ʿāmma The hospital was not financed with public money.

Agent; strictly speaking not possible in Arabic, but some newspapers imitate foreign practice, using the compound preposition من (قبل) *min (qibali)* 'on the part of' :

أُقترح العلاج من (قبل) منظّمة الصحّة العالمية.

uqtúriḥ al-ʿilāj min (qibal) munaẓẓamat aṣ-ṣiḥḥa l-ʿālamīya.

The treatment was proposed by the World Health Organisation.

Many still, however, prefer an active tense for this kind of sentence:

اقترحت العلاج منظّمة .... *iqtàrahat al-ʿilāj munaẓẓamat ...*

The W.H.O. proposed the treatment.

In Chapter 13 we study an alternative structure with similar emphasis.

Agreement; the passive verb agrees normally with its subject where that subject would be the direct object (B 12) of the active verb:

جُرح شخصان في الانفجار. *juriḥ shakhṣān fi l-infijār.*

Two people were injured in the blast.

But where the object of the active verb is *prepositional*, the passive is impersonal, and always stands in the masc. sing. (like the participle):

يفتّش عن متخصّصي القلب. *yufattash ʿan mutakhaṣṣiṣi l-qalb.*

Heart specialists are being sought.

يقام ببرامج تلقيح. *yuqām bi-barāmij talqīḥ.*

Vaccination programmes are being undertaken.

This impersonal use is found also with verbs not taking an object at all:

تُردّد بسبب ضغط الدم. *turuddid bi-sabab ḍaghṭ ad-dam.* There was hesitation ('It was hesitated') because of the blood pressure.

4. Passive tense and passive participle

Compare two passive sentences, one with a tense, one with a participle as predicate (B 27):

يُلقّح ألوف من الناس. *yulaqqaḥ 'ulūf min an-nās.*

Thousands of people are being vaccinated.

ألوف من الناس ملقّحون. *'ulūf min an-nās mulaqqaḥūn.*
Thousands of people are vaccinated.

Both are present in time. But the tense indicates an *action*: people are being vaccinated (now), whereas the participle shows a *state*: people are (now) vaccinated (= in a vaccinated state).

5. Vocabulary: الصحّة *aṣ-ṣiḥḥa* **Health**

(طبيب\جرّاح) بيطاري *(ṭabīb/jarrāḥ) baiṭārī* veterinary (doctor/surgeon)
ترشّح *tarashshaḥa* V to catch a cold
تعالج *ta'ālaja* VI to undergo treatment
جرثوم\جرثومة جراثيم *jurthūm(a) jarāthīm* germ, microbe
جرح يجرح *jaraḥa yajraḥu* I to injure
جسم أجسام *jism 'ajsām* body
حرارة *ḥarāra* fever, temperature, heat
حقن يقحن *ḥaqana yaqḥunu* I to inject
خقنة حقن *ḥuqna ḥuqan* injection
دخّن *dakhkhana* II to smoke
درجة حرارة *darajat ḥarāra* temperature
دواء أدوية *dawā' 'ádwiya* medicine, medication
رشح *rashḥ* a cold
سالم *sālim* healthy
سنّ أسنان *sinn 'asnān* tooth
صدر صدور *ṣadr ṣudūr* chest
صيدلي صيادلة *ṣaidalī ṣayādila* pharmacist
صيدلية *ṣaidalīya* pharmacy
ضغط ضغوط *ḍaghṭ ḍughūṭ* pressure
طبيب أسنان *ṭabīb 'asnān* dentist
ظهر ظهور *ẓahr ẓuhūr* back
عاجز عجزة *'ājiz 'ajaza* disabled

عالج *ʿālaja* III to treat, to cure
عجز *ʿajz* disability
قلب قلوب *qalb qulūb* heart
كبير\صغير *kabīr/ṣaghīr* (also:) old/young.
لقّح (ضدّ) *laqqaḥa* II *(ḍidd)* to vaccinate (against)
ماء الشرب\للشرب *mā' ash-shurb/li-sh-shurb* drinking water
مجروح مجاريح *majrūḥ majārīḥ* injured
مرشّح *murashshaḥ* (also:) having a cold
مرض يمرض *maraḍa yamraḍu* I to fall ill
مرض أمراض *maraḍ 'amrāḍ* disease
مريض مرضى *marīḍ marḍa* sick
نظافة *niẓāfa* cleanness
نظّف *naẓẓafa* II to clean
نظيف نظفاء *naẓīf nuẓafā'* clean
وجع أوجاع *wajaʿ 'awjāʿ* pain
وجع يوجع* *wajiʿa yawjaʿu* I to be painful, to feel pain
وساخة *wasākha* dirt
وسّخ *wassakha* II to soil
وسخ *wasikh* dirty
ولادة *wilāda* birth

(* NB irregular; initial root letter و is kept in the active present tense)

Exercise 1. Complete, with the verb in the passive, past tense and present tense:

e.g.: *kutibat/tuktab ar-risāla*..(كتب) الرسالة.←كُتبت\تُكتب الرسالة

١ (عالج) الطفل المريض. ٢ (تردّد) في تطبيق العلاج.
٣ (اقترح) عملية جراحية. ٤ (اشترى) الدواء في الصيدلية.
٥ (انسحب) من هذا الوضع. ٦ (أعلن) التفاصيل فوراً.
٧ (فاوض) الميزانية الصحّية. ٨ (بحث) وضع المريض.
٩ إنّ الطلبات (رفض). ١٠ إنّ الطلبين (رفض).

Exercise 2. Re-express the sentence, using a passive tense:

e.g.: خفّضوا درجة الحرارة. ← خُفِّضت درجة الحرارة.

khuffiḍat darajat al-ḥarāra.

١ وقّعا النشرة الطبّية بعد بحث طويل.
٢ يفاوضون شروط دفع الضمان الاجتماعي.
٣ استغنوا عن كلّ تدخّل جرّاحي.
٤ يستعملون علاجًا جديداً وغاليًا ضدّ أمراض الدم.
٥ انسحبوا من المنطقة لعدم وجود ماء نظيف للشرب.
٦ قرّروا في الأخبار أنّ المرض لا يزال يتوسّع في جنوب البلاد.
٧ اكتشفوا الجرثوم قبل أكثر من مئتي سنة.
٨ طبّقوا إجراءات استثنائية لمكافحة أمراض الأطفال الصغار.
٩ لم يستفيدوا كثيراً من العملية المقوم بها.
١٠ يؤكّدون في صحافة اليوم وضع المجاريح.

Exercise 3. Complete the sentence with your own words. The sentence must contain one passive tense:

e.g.: ووفق على العلاج ... ← ...الّذي تحتاج إليه المريضة.

wūfiq ʿala l-ʿilāj alladhī taḥtāj ʾilayhi l-marīḍa.

١ أُكّد في النشرة الطبّية ... ٢ عُلم أمس من بغداد ...
٣ يُشكّ في ... ٤ ... حول الوضع الصحّي في الريف
٥ ... ارتفاع تكاليف العلاج ٦ أُستقبل وفد ...
٧ نشروا موجز تقرير أُعلن فيه ... ٨ ... في بطبيق الإجراء

Exercise 4. Complete with a passive tense, (a) past and (b) present:

e.g.: *kutibat/tuktab ar-risāla.* ... الرسالة ← كُتبت\تُكتب الرسالة.

١ ... أرقام التقرير. ٢ ... على تفاصيل البرنامج اليوم.
٣ كيف ... هذه الماكينة؟ ٤ لم ... من المسؤول.
٥ هل ... الخطّة أم لا؟ ٦ ... على اقتراح الأمين العامّ.
٧ ... أسماء المرشّحين الناجحين. ٨ ... إجراءات خلال الأزمة.
٩ ... استبدال الآلات القديمة. ١٠ ... وسائل مختلفة لحلّ مشكلتنا.

7 Words – 6

- Quadriliteral verbs

1. General

All the verbs so far studied are triliteral, i.e. they have a root of three letters. A few verbs, some of them important, are quadriliteral, i.e. have a root of four letters. Note, with regard to quadriliteral verbs:

- Most are sound. Any weak root letter (و\ي) stabilises into a consonant *w/y*, and the verb follows the sound pattern.
- Tenses and personal prefixes and endings are as for triliteral verbs.
- Only Forms I and II (which we shall label IQ and IIQ) are common and need concern us.

2. Form IQ

Model is ترجم يترجم *tarjama yutarjimu* IQ 'to translate' (root ترجم). In everything except the verbal noun it follows the pattern of triliteral Form II (see B 20), if we treat the second and third quadriliteral root letters as equal to the doubled middle root letter of the triliteral pattern. Compare:

علّم يعلم	*'allama yu'allimu* II	to teach
ترجم يترجم	*tarjama yutarjimu* IQ	to translate

Past tense:

ترجمت *tarjamtu*, ترجمت *tarjamta*, ترجمت *tarjamti*,
ترجم *tarjama*, ترجمت *tarjamat*;
ترجمنا *tarjamna*, ترجمتوا *tarjamtū*, ترجموا *tarjamū*
Dual ترجمتما *tarjamtuma*, ترجما *tarjama*, ترجمتا *tarjamata*
Fem. pl. ترجمتّن *tarjamtunna*, ترجمن *tarjamna*

هل ترجموا تقرير المحاكمة؟ *hal tarjamū taqrīr al-muḥākama?*
Have they translated the report of the trial?

Present tense:

أترجم *'utarjimu*, تترجم *tutarjimu*, تترجمين *tutarjimīna*,
يترجم *yutarjimu*, تترجم *tutarjimu*;
نترجم *nutarjimu*, تترجمون *tutarjimūna*, يترجمون *yutarjimūna*
Dual تترجمان *tutarjimāni*, يترجمن *yutarjimāni*,
تترجمان *tutarjimāni*
Fem. pl. تترجمن *tutarjimna*, يترجمن *yutarjimna*

سنترجمه بعد إصدار الحكم. *sa-nutarjimuhu ba'd 'iṣdār al-ḥukm*. We will translate it after pronouncement ('issue') of sentence.

Subjunctive and Jussive: as for triliteral sound Form II, see B 23:

يحاولون أن يترجموا قضيةً معقّدةً. *yuḥāwilūna 'an yutarjimū qaḍīya mu'aqqada*. They are trying to translate a difficult case.

لم أترجمه بعد. *lam 'utarjimhu ba'd*. I have not yet translated it.

Imperative: ترجم *tarjim*, ترجمي *tarjimī*; ترجموا *tarjimū*
Dual ترجما *tarjima*; Fem. pl. ترجمن *tarjimna*

Participles: Active مترجم *mutarjim*, Passive مترجم *mutarjam*

Passive tenses(هو): past ترجم *turjima*, present يترجم *yutarjamu*

Vb. noun: irregular: for this verb it is ترجمة تراجم *tarjama tarājim*.

Other important verbs in Form IQ, with their verbal nouns:

برهن على *barhana 'ala* to prove	برهان براهين *burhān barāhīn* proof
سلسل *salsala* to connect	سلسلة سلاسل *silsila salāsil* chain, series
زلزل *zalzala* to shake, rock	زلزال *zilzāl* shaking, earthquake
سيطر على *sayṭara 'ala* to rule over	سيطرة *sayṭara* rule
دحرج *daḥraja* to roll (something)	دحرجة *daḥraja* roll(ing)
فلسف *falsafa* to philosophise	فلسفة *falsafa* philosophy
تلفز *talfaza* to televise	تلفزة *talfaza* television
تلفن *talfana* to telephone	(verbal noun not used)

3. Form IIQ

Form IIQ often expresses the complementary action of IQ. Form IIQ follows in all respects the pattern of triliteral Form V, *including* the regular formation of the verbal noun, if we regard the second and third quadriliteral root letters as equal to the doubled middle root letter of the triliteral verb. Compare:

تعلّم *ta'allama* V to learn
تسلسل *tasalsala* IIQ to form a chain or sequence

Past tense (هو): تسلسل *tasalsala*
Present tense (هو): يتسلسل *yatasalsalu*
Imperative (rare): تسلسل\ي\وا *tasalsal/ī/ū*
Active participle: متسلسل *mutasalsil* consecutive
ثلاث قضايا متسلسلة *thalāth qaḍāya mutasalsila* three consecutive cases
Verbal noun: تسلسل *tasalsul* sequence, succession
تسلسل اتّهامات غير صحيحة *tasalsul ittihāmāt ghayr ṣaḥīḥa* a sequence of untrue accusations

so also, in Form IIQ:

توشوش *tawashwasha* to whisper
تزلزل *tazalzala* to quake (especially of the earth)
تدحرج *tadaḥraja* to roll (itself)
تأمرك *ta'amraka* to be(come) Americanised

Passive (tenses and participle): none

4. Vocabulary: الحقوق *al-ḥuqūq* Jurisprudence

اتّهم (ب) *ittáhama* VIII *(bi)* to accuse (of)
أثبت *'athbata* IV to prove
أدان *'adāna* IV to convict
ارتكب *irtákaba* VIII to perpetrate
استغلّ *istaghalla* X to exploit
أصدر *'aṣdara* IV to issue, declare, pronounce
بريء أبرياء (من) *barī' 'abriyā' (min)* innocent (of)

جرم أجرام *jurm 'ajrām* offence
جنائي *jinā'ī* criminal (case, law etc.)
الحقّ عليه *al-ḥaqq 'alayhi* he is (in the) wrong
الحق معه *al-ḥaqq ma'ahu* he is (in the) right
حكم أحكام *ḥukm 'aḥkām* judgment, rule
حكم يحكم على *ḥakama yaḥkumu* I *'ala* to judge, sentence
دستور دساتير *dustūr dasātīr* constitution, statute
دعوى دعاوى *da'wa da'āwa* case, lawsuit
رفض يرفض *rafaḍa yarfiḍu* I (also:) to dismiss (a case)
زوّر *zawwara* II to falsify
سرق يسرق *saraqa yasriqu* I to steal
سرقة *sariqa* theft
الشريعة *ash-sharī'a* Sharia (Muslim) law
شهادة *shahāda* (also:) testimony, evidence
شهد يشهد (ب\أنّ) *shahida yashhadu* I *(bi-, 'anna)* to testify
صحيح صحاح *ṣaḥīḥ ṣiḥāḥ* true, correct
ضرر أضرار *ḍarar 'aḍrār* damage
ضرّ يضرّ *ḍarra yaḍurru* I to damage
عدل *'adl* just, fair
عدلية *'adlīya* justice
عقوبة *'uqūba* punishment
على علم ب *'ala 'ilm bi-* aware of
قاتل قتّال *qātil quttāl* killer, murderer
قتل *qatl* murder, homicide
قتل يقتل *qatala yaqtulu* I to kill, murder
قذف *qadhf* libel, slander
كذب يكذب *kadhaba yakdhibu* I to tell a lie
كذب أكذاب *kidhb 'akdhāb* lie
لصّ لصوص *liṣṣ luṣūṣ* thief

مدّع\المدّعي *mudda'in, al-mudda'ī* (weak) plaintiff, prosecutor

(الـ)مدّعى عليه *mudda'an, al-mudda'a* (weak) *'alayhi* defendant

مدني *madanī* civil (case, law, engineering etc.)

مذنب *mudhnib* guilty

نصح ينصح (ل ب) *naṣaḥa yanṣaḥu* I (*li-* person, *bi-* thing) to advise

ورث يرث *waritha yarithu* I to inherit

ورث *wirth* inheritance

وريث ورثاء *warīth wurathā'* heir

Exercise 1. Put into the present tense:

e.g.: قد ترجموا التقرير. ← يترجمون التقرير. *yutarjimūna t-taqrīr.*

١ تلفزنا كلّ الأخبار. ٢ أصدرت المحكمة حكمها.

٣ برهن الشاهد على حقيقة شهادته. ٤ أُتّهم بالسرقة.

٥ هل تلفن أحد من وزارة العدلية؟

Exercise 2. Answer:

e.g.: ما هو دستور دولة؟ ←الدستور هو قانون الدولة الأساسي.

ad-dustūr huwa qānūn ad-dawla l-'asāsī.

١ اشرح الفرق بين دعوى مدني ودعوى جنائي.

٢ اذكر مثل دعوى مدني.

٣ ما هي دور شاهد؟

٤ اذكر دفاعًا مقبولاً على اتّهام القذف.

٥ أيّة من الجريمتين أشدّ، السرقة أو القتل؟

٦ لا يقول الشاهد الحقّ. إنّه ....

٧ لماذا من الضروري أن كلّ شاهد يقول الحقّ؟

٨ أيّ مبدأ يجب أن يأخذ القاضي بعين الاعتبار من أجل تقدير مبلغ التعويض في دعوى أضرار ماديّة؟

٩ لا يعرف المدعى عليه لغة المحكمة (العربية مثلاً). اقترح حلاً لهذا الوضع.
١٠ يبرهن المدّعى عليه في قضية قذف على أنّ قوله صحيح. هل يجب على القاضي أن يرفض الدعوى؟

Exercise 3. Under what entry in a root-based dictionary do we find:

e.g.: مدّعون ← دعو

١ مقررون ٢ يتفلسف ٣ مذنب ٤ ادّعاء
٥ زارت ٦ تأخّرنا ٧ تأمركنا ٨ مستشفيات
٩ المستثناه ١٠ ثانوية ١١ ترجعوا ١٢ ترجموا

Exercise 4. Read the passage and answer the questions:

المادّة(1) ١١ من الإعلان العالمي(2) لحقوق الإنسان

(١) كلّ شخص متّهم بجريمة يُعتبر بريئًا إلى أن تُثبت إدانته قانونيًا بمحكمة علنية(3) تؤمّن له فيها الضمانات الضرورية للدفاع عنه.

(٢) لا يدان أيّ شخص من جراء(4) قيامه بفعل أو عدم قيامه بفعل ألاّ إذا كان ذلك يُعتبر جرمًا وفقًا(5) للقانون الوطني أو الدولي وقت الارتكاب، كذلك لا توقّع(6) عليه عقوبة أشدّ من تلك التّي كان يجوز توقيعها وقت ارتكاب الجرم.

(Article 11 of the UN Universal Declaration of Human Rights)

(1) مادّة موادّ (here:) clause, article (2) عالمي (here:) universal

(3) علني *'alanī* public (4) من جراء *min jarā'* on account of

(5) وفقًا لـ *wafqan li-* pursuant to, in conformity with

(6) وقّع (على) II (here:) to impose (e.g. a penalty) (on)

١ هل يجب على المتّهم أن يثبت أنّه بريء؟
٢ اشرح مثلاً تطبيق أول المبدئين المذكورين تحت الرقم ٢.
٣ حسب الأمم المتّحده الإعلان قابل للتطبيق في كلّ بلدان العالم. هل يمكن هذا التطبيق العالمي، بالفعل؟ اشرح رأيك.

8 Revision – 1

- Words

Exercise 1. Add the parenthesised expression as object of the verb:

e.g.: أصدر القاضي (حكم خفيف). ← أصدر القاضي حكمًا خفيفًا.

'aṣdar al-qāḍī ḥukman khafīfan.

١ وظّفوا (أخ أصغر). ٢ وظّفوا (أخوه الأصغر).
٣ رأينا (زميلان سابقان) في المعرض.
٤ يقدّمون (اقترحات أخرى) لتسوية الخلاف مع النقابة.
٥ رأينا (زملاء أجانب) في المعرض.
٦ لم نذكر إلاّ (مبدأ واحد) وهو الحقّ في ماء الشرب.
٧ تترجم السكرتيرة (تقارير ورسالات).
٨ إنّي عرفت (أب) هذا الطبيب عندما درست في الجامعة.
٩ أشترين (خبز وملح وزبدة وفواكه) للعشاء.
١٠ يعلب تقدير ربح وخسارة (دور أساسي) في اختيارنا.

Exercise 2. Give the opposite of the word or expression:

e.g.: *al-muddaʿa ʿalayhi* المدّعى عليه ← المدّعِي

١ رجل	٢ مملكة	٣ قريب من	٤ وقف
٥ خسر	٦ انساني	٧ مريض	٨ عزل
٩ الحق معنا	١٠ وبخ	١١ تقريبًا	١٢ يقول الحق

Exercise 3. Under what entry in a root-based dictionary do we find:

e.g.: كانت ← كون

١ يرجعون	٢ يرجون	٣ جرت	٤ جرّاح
٥ محلول	٦ زرنا	٧ نام	٨ نامية
٩ تدحرجت	١٠ متّحد	١١ مترجمون	١٢ يابان

Exercise 4. Substitute the word given for the corresponding word in the sentence preceding it (making any other necessary changes):

e.g.: وصل اليوم النجّار بآلاته. (جاء)
← جاء اليوم النجّار بآلاته. (رجع)
← رجع اليوم النجّار بآلاته. (etc.)

سمعنا شهادة التاجر.
١ (درس) ٢ (رفض) ٣ (سجّل) ٤ (كتب)

أضرب النقّاشون لعدم تعويض تكاليفهم.
٥ (سبّاك) ٦ (عامل) ٧ (زميل) ٨ (محام)

Now do this chain substitution. Substitute the word given, in the right place in the sentence preceding it (making any other necessary changes).

e.g.: وصل اليوم النجّار بآلاته. (منشار)
← وصل اليوم النجّار بمنشاره. (جاء)
← جاء اليوم النجّار بمنشاره. (etc.)

عالج الطبيب المريض بواسطة دواء جديد.
٩ (البنت) ١٠ (ساعد) ١١ (علاج) ١٢ (الممرّضة)

للفطور يتناول الضيوف عادةً بيضًا وقهوةً.
١٣ (فواكه) ١٤ (دائمًا) ١٥ (غداء) ١٦ (عصير)
١٧ (لبن) ١٨ (أمّي) ١٩ (كلّ يوم) ٢٠ (يأمر)

إنّ سكّان القرية اجتمعوا في البلدية من أجل بحث هامّ.
٢١ (جلس) ٢٢ (الشيوخ) ٢٣ (مكتب) ٢٤ (your choice)

Now do the whole of Exercise 4 again, *faster*.

Exercise 5. Make the verbs and suffixes (a) masc. dual, (b) fem. dual and (c) fem. plural. Make other changes as needed:

e.g.: رأوا أخاهم ← رأيا أخاهما ، رأتا أخاهما ، رأين أخاهنّ
ra'aya 'akhāhuma, ra'ata 'akhāhuma, ra'ayna 'akhāhunna

١ تأخر لأنّه قد زار صديقه المريض في المستشفى العامّ.
٢ احتجّ على قوله. ٣ يهتمّون بأطفالهم.
٤ تريد (هي) أن تساعدها. ٥ كان شاهداً في المحكمة.

٦ طلبوا مساعدة أصدقائهم الأقرب في وضعهم الصعب.
٧ يستعمل معرفته للغة العربية في شغله الفنّي.
٨ لا تنسى أن تذكر اسمك عندما تطلب الكتب المحجوزة لك.

Do the same with nouns, pronouns and demonstratives:

٩ هذا هو الطبيب الّذي يستطيع أن يساعده.
١٠ أن الشاهد حاول أن يكذب في حكايته.

Exercise 6. Use the word or expression in a sentence which indicates its meaning:

e.g.: قاض ← أصدر القاضي حكمًا شديداً.

'aṣdar al-qāḍī ḥukman shadīdan.

١ انقلاب	٢ مؤهّل	٣ استوصف	٤ ممرّضة
٥ أدار	٦ ربح يربح	٧ مفاوضة	٨ ترجم
٩ مريض	١٠ قلب	١١ كتب يكتب	١٢ تلفزة

Exercise 7. Give the (a) active participle (m. sing.), (b) passive participle if any (m. sing.), and (c) verbal noun (sing.):

e.g.: اتّهم ← متّهِم، متّهَم، اتّهام

muttáhim, muttáham, ittihām

١ برهن	٢ استوصف	٣ كان	٤ اعتمد على
٥ أعان	٦ رخّص	٧ نوى	٨ أصدر
٩ تناول	١٠ استقال	١١ قرأ	١٢ تقاعد

Exercise 8. Use each word or expression, in the form shown, in a sentence:

e.g.: *hal ta'rif 'abā zamīlika?* أبا ← هل تعرف أبا زميلك؟

١ جهودها	٢ متزوجون	٣ المدعى عليهم	٤ الجرّاحين
٥ أبو	٦ التدريب المهني	٧ الاجتماعية	٨ اجتماعات
٩ لليهود	١٠ محدودة	١١ اخوان	١٢ قابلة ل

Exercise 9. Give the second principle part of each verb, and the singular of each noun or adjective:

e.g.: *kātib* كاتب ← كتّاب

١ صحاح	٢ جهود	٣ حكم	٤ خسر
٥ منح	٦ شيوخ	٧ فقراء	٨ برهن
٩ عزل	١٠ مثاقب	١١ استقال	١٢ أنظمة

Exercise 10. Re-express the verb in the passive, omitting any agent:

e.g.: *'u'lin* أُعلن ← أعلنوه

١ حكم عليهم	٢ عالجوه	٣ يضرّونها	٤ ترجمناه
٥ يسرقه	٦ تلفزوه أمس	٧ اتّهموا	٨ تناولوها

Exercise 11. Begin each sentence with a suitable and different passive verb, in the (a) past tense and (b) present tense:

e.g.: ... أنّ العملية نجحت. ← أُعلن\يعلن أنّ العملية نجحت.

'u'lin/yu'lan 'inna l-'amalīya najaḥat.

١ ... في إفادة مثل هذا الدفاع أمام هذا القاضي.
٢ ... كيف يتطوّر الوضع الطبّي لزملائنا المجاريح.
٣ ... هذا التقرير على برنامج آخر، أظنّ.
٤ ... خلال العملية انخفاض الضغط.
٥ ... شديداً على اقتراح المختار وشيوخ القرية.
٦ ... فوراً باستئناف سلسلة فحوص طبيّة عند السكّان.

Exercise 12. Re-express, avoiding the compound adjective or noun:

e.g.: مسألة قابل لاهتمامنا ← مسألة يجب أن نهتمّ بها

mas'ala yajib 'an nahtamm biha

١ شخص عديم فهم الأمر	٢ كبار الموظّفين
٣ النصّ الألماني - العربي	٤ النتائج غير قابلة للشرح
٥ التقرير نصف السنوي	٦ سياسات مختلف الأحزاب

٧ فشل البرنامج لعدم الاستثمار الكافي.

9 Structures – 1

- Accusative

1. General

The accusative (النصب) is by far the most versatile of the three cases. We have studied it in various uses :

- direct object of a verb (B 12):

  عقد بوليصةً شاملةً. *(būlīṣatan shāmilatan)*

  He took ('concluded') a comprehensive policy.

- time expressions with no preposition (B 12, 39):

  صباحًا in the morning

- after كم (B 13): كم طرفًا ؟ How many parties?
- predicate of one of the sisters of كان (B 18):

  كان الحريق واسعًا. *(al-ḥarīq)* The fire was extensive.

- after لا in 'there is no ...' or إلاّ in affirmative exceptions (B 23):

  لا بندَ أوضح في العقد كلّه. *(lā banda 'awḍaḥ)*

  There is no clearer article in the whole contract.

  احتجّ الكلّ إلاّ المأمورين. All protested except the officials.

- comparative of derived adjectives (B 29):

  أكثر تعقيدًا more complicated

- subject of a verb after one of the sisters of أنّ (B 31):

  لأنّ مسؤوليته محدودة. *(mas'ūliyatahu)*

  because its liability is limited

- simple adverbs (B 32): دائمًا always
- with indefinite numbers 11 to 99 (B 38):

  ٥٠ جنيهًا مصريًا £ 50 Egyptian

Chapter 13 of this manual examines one further important use of the accusative, in so-called expressions of circumstance.

Other important accusative expressions are examined below.

2. Absolute object

Examine the following expression:

يشرحونه شرحًا طويلاً. They are explaining it at length.
('explaining it a long explanation')

The manner in which the verb is executed is expressed with a verbal noun from the same root (not necessarily the same form I-X), in the indefinite accusative, with an adjective indicating the manner. This is called the *absolute object* (المفعول المطلق *al-maf'ūl al-muṭlaq*).

The verb may be one not normally taking a direct object:

يحتجّون احتجاجًا شديدًا. They are protesting strongly
('protesting a strong protest').

شككنا فيه شكًّا عميقًا. ('We doubted in it a deep doubt')
We doubted it profoundly.

Other variants of absolute object are:

- adjective replaced by an expression with a similar function, e.g. a construct (B 7) or a distributive (B 9):

  سيهتم به اهتمام أخ. He will look after him like a brother
  ('(with) a brother's care').

  يخافونه* كلّ الخوف. They have ('fear') every fear of it.

  (* here the verb has both its own object and an absolute object.)

- (less common) no adjective, with the implicit idea 'completely':

  انقلبوا انقلابًا. *inqálabu nqilāban.*
  They were completely overthrown.

English has the absolute object only in set expressions: 'He laughed a hollow laugh.' In Arabic, it is a standard structure, though now less common than the simple adverbial accusative shown in B 32.

3. Adverbial phrases

Some adverbial expressions consist of a verbal noun in the indefinite accusative form followed by a preposition. We have already learned

ابتداءً\اعتباراً من 'with effect/starting from', and وفقاً ل 'pursuant to, in conformity with' (from وفق *wafq* 'conformity'). Other examples are:

تأييداً ل *ta'yīdan li-* in support of

عملاً ب *'amalan bi-* in accordance with, pursuant to

خوفاً من\على *khawfan min* for fear of; *khawfan 'ala* fearing for

رغبةً في *raghbatan fī* aiming at, wishing for (رغبة I wish)

إجابةً ل *'ijābatan li-* in response to (إجابة IV response)

إكراماً ل *'ikrāman li-* in honour of (إكرام IV deference)

بناءً على *binā'an 'ala* on the basis of (بناء I construction)

تمهيداً ل *tamhīdan li-* preparatory to (تمهيد II preparation)

نظراً إلى\ل *naẓaran 'ila/li-* in view of, with a view to (نظر I view)

نيابةً عن *niyābatan 'an* deputising for, in place of (نيابة I replacement, deputyship)

4. Expressions of place

Note also accusative expressions of *place* with no preposition, e.g.:

يساراً\يميناً *yasāran, yamīnan* (= على اليسار\اليمين) on the left/right

شمالاً *shimālan* (= في الشمال) in the north

5. As

Note the accusative in expressions of the type

بصفته سمساراً *bi-ṣifatihi simsāran* in his capacity as broker

(بـ)وظيفتي مؤمّناً *(bi-)waẓīfatī mu'amminan* (in) my job as insurer

6. ... إيّا *'iyyā-*

A few verbs can take two direct objects. When we wish to express both direct objects as pronouns, the second pronoun object is suffixed not to the verb but to the separate particle ... إيّا *'iyyā-*:

أعطونا البوليصة. They gave us the policy.

أعطونا إيّاها. *('iyyāha)* They gave it to us.
لم يسألوه رأيه. They did not ask him his opinion.
لم يسألوه إيّاه. *('iyyāhu)* They did not ask him for it.

7. Elliptical expressions

A direct object whose verb is understood and omitted, stands (as is logical) in the accusative:

(أقدّم) شكراً. *shukran.* (I offer) Thanks.
(أطلب) عفواً. *'afwan.* (I ask) Pardon.

8. Complement

Examine these sentences where a noun or adjective not only qualifies the direct object of the verb, but completes the action of the verb itself:

أعتبر هذا الشخص† صديقاً*. *(ṣadīqan)*
I consider this person (to be/as) a friend.
نجدهم كلّهم† مسؤولين*. *(mas'ūlīn)* We find all of them responsible.
عيّنوه† رئيساً*. *'ayyanūhu ra'īsan.*
They appointed him (to be) chairman.

The adjective or noun (*) qualifying or identifying the direct-object noun or pronoun (†) is called a *complement*. Note that the complement stands in the *indefinite* accusative form.

9. Exclamations

'How ...!' is expressed with ما + the comparative adjective in the accusative; any explicit pronoun subject is suffixed to the adjective:

ما أطول هذه الاستمارة. *(istimāra)* How long this form is.
ما أطولها. *mā 'aṭwalaha.* How long it is.

We can also use كم + a short nominal sentence:

كم هذا معقّد. How complicated this is.

For an adverb + verb, we repeat ما:

ما أوضح ما يشرحونه. How clearly they explain it.

'How much/many ...!' is of course كم or كم من :

كم وقتًا\من الوقت خسرنا . How much time we have lost.

10. Vocabulary: التأمين *at-ta'mīn* Insurance

احترق *iḥtáraqa* VIII to burn, be on fire

أحرق *'aḥraqa* IV to burn, set on fire

ادّعى *idda'a* VIII (also:) to claim

بند بنود *band bunūd* clause, article, paragraph

بوليصة بواليص *būlīṣa bawālīṣ* policy

تأمين ضدّ الحريق\الحوادث\السريقة\الأضرار\الفيضان\الغير *ta'mīn ḍidd al-ḥarīq/al-ḥawādith/as-sarīqa/al-'aḍrār/al-fayaḍān/al-ghayr* fire/accident/theft/damage/flood/third party insurance

تأمين على الحياة *ta'mīn 'ala l-ḥayā* life insurance

تصادف *taṣādafa* VI to happen by chance; *taṣāduf* coincidence

تصادم (ب\مع) *taṣādama* VI *(bi-, ma')* to collide (with); *taṣādum* collision

تنازل عن (ل) *tanāzala* VI *'an* (thing) *(li-)* (person) to renounce (in favour of); to waive; *tanāzul ('an)* waiver (of)

حادث حوادث *ḥādith ḥawādith* accident

حريق حرائق *ḥarīq ḥarā'iq* fire

خطر أخطار *khaṭar 'akhṭār* danger, risk

سمسار سماسير *simsār samāsīr* broker

شامل *shāmil* comprehensive

صاحب أصحاب *ṣāḥib 'aṣḥāb* holder, owner

طبيعي *ṭabī'ī* natural

طرف ثالث *ṭaraf thālith* third party

فاض يفيض *fāḍa yafīḍu* I to flood

فرع فروع *far' furū'* branch
قسط أقساط *qisṭ 'aqsāṭ* premium
كارثة كوارث *kāritha kawārith* disaster
مستفيد *mustafīd* beneficiary
مسؤولية *mas'ūlīya* (also:) liability
ملك يملك *malaka yamliku* I to own
ملك أملاك *milk 'amlāk* property
نموذج *namūdhaj* model; form (document)

Exercise 1. Add an absolute object qualified as shown:

e.g.: *iqtaraḥ iqtirāḥan fannīyan*.. اقترح (فنّي) ← اقترح اقتراحًا فنّيًا

١ مرضَت (خطر) ٢ سيرفضون طلبك (شديد)
٣ تنازل السمسار (واسع) ٤ تصادم بسيّارة جاره (خفيف)
٥ تعرف الموضوع (خبير) ٦ أمّنوا البناية (تامّ)
٧ شرحت اقتراحها (كلّ) ٨ جاوب الزائر (طفل) على سؤالي

Exercise 2. Complete the sentence with an adverbial expression, with alternative answers where appropriate:

e.g.: إنّ البوليصة مقدّمة ... طلب الزبون. ← إجابةً ل\وفقًا ل

'inna l-būlīṣa muqaddama 'ijābatan li-/wafqan li-ṭalab az-zabūn.

١ حضّر الوثائق ... المفاوضات. ٢ يقود الوفد ... مديرنا.
٣ ... ذلك يجب رفض الاقتراح. ٤ تردّدنا ... خسارة كبيرة.
٥ اجتمع الزملاء ...ك. ٦ تردّدنا ... نجاح مفاضاتنا.
٧ ألقى خطابًا ... الحزب الجديد. ٨ نرسل طلبًا للوزير ... تأييده.

Exercise 3. Complete the 'as' expression:

e.g.: *waẓīfatuha mumarriḍatan* وظيفتها (ممرّضة)← وظيفتها ممرّضةً

١ خارج مهمّتي (سمسار) ٢ بصفتهم (خبراء)
٣ بصفتهم (مساعد فنّي) ٤ في دورك (نائب مدير)
٥ بصفتنا (زملاؤك) ٦ في حدود أهليته (حفّار)

Exercise 4. Enlarge this form (125%) and fill it in as an applicant:

نموذج أ\٢٨٤ شركة "الوطن" المحدودة للتأمين

نموذج طلب تأمين منزل

(وفقًا لنظام التأمين لسنة ٢٠٠٥)

١ بيانات طالب التأمين (= ساكن المنزل ومستفيد البوليصة)

الاسم الكامل .... تاريخ الولادة ....

عنوان المنزل .... التلفون ....

صاحب\ مستأجر المنزل المذكور؟ .... مدّة الاستئجار ......

التأمين مطلوب ضدّ أخطار ....

المهنة والوظيفة .... العائلة ....

صاحب العمل .... منذ سنة .....

وثائق مقدّمة تأييداً لهذا الطلب (إن وُجدت) ....

٢ بيانات المنزل

النوع (بيت، شقّة أو غيره) .... عدد السكّان الدائمين ....

عدد غرف .... مطبخ؟ .... كاراج؟ .... قيمة حالية .... دينار

سنة البناء .... لأيّ غرض يُستعمل المنزل؟ ....

تفاصيل أخرى ....

٣ بيانات صاحب المنزل

الاسم الكامل ....

العنوان والتلفون ....

٤ شهادة إنّني على علم ببنود شروط العامّة لشركة "الوطن" وأشهد بحقيقة جميع المعلومات المذكورة في هذا الطلب حسب معرفتي.

توقيع طالب التأمين .... المكان والتاريخ ....

(لاستعمال مسؤولي الشركة فقط)

رقم الطلب .... الفرع .... تاريخ الاستلام ....

رأي السمسار: قابل للقبول\ للرفض بناءً على (أساس الرأي) ....

....

اسم وتوقيع السمسار .... التاريخ ....

القسط الكامل .... شهريًا \ (نصف) سنويًا ، ابتداءً من ....

قرار وتوقيع مفتّش العامّ .... التاريخ ....

Now you are the broker, and you recommend acceptance. Fill in the company's part of the form. Sign both for yourself and the (absent) inspector general; annotate that you are deputising for the latter.

Exercise 5. Re-express the noun direct objects as suffixes:

e.g.: *nu'allimuhum 'iyyāha.* نعلّم التلاميذ الهندسة. ← نعلّمهم إيّاها.

١ أعطاني العقد. ٢ سنري الممثّلين الأساليب.
٣ سألونا نفس التفاصيل. ٤ لم يعطوا السمسار النصّ.
٥ إنّ قسم التعويض لم يمنح الزبون المبلغ المطلوب.

Exercise 6. Complete the sentence with the complement shown:

e.g.: *'aẓunnuhu mas'ūlan.* أظنّه (مسؤول). ← أظنّه مسؤولاً.

١ أعتبرها (بنت لطيفة). ٢ هل تجده (زميل طيّب)؟
٣ انّنا نعتبر التعويض (كاف)، ٤ ... وأعتبره أنا (غير كاف).
٥ كيف تجد العقد؟ - (معقّد). ٦ لم يعتبروه (أهمّ مشكلة).

Exercise 7. Define:

e.g.: *'aqd 'aw wathīqat ta'mīn* بوليصة ← عقد أو وثيقة تأمين

١ سمسار ٢ تعويض ٣ تأمين شامل ٤ طرف ثالث
٥ صاحب بيت ٦ مستفيد ٧ قسط ٨ المستأجر

Exercise 8. Collect together words having the same root:

e.g.: أمن، تأمين، مؤمّن. أخر، متأخّر، ...

مطار وقّع سنة قاضى صادرات حرائق طيران تعقيد افاد اصدار احترق
موقّع سنويًا يطير احرق معقد فائدة عقود قد استفاد قضية يفيد توقيع

10 Structures – 2

- Expressions with verb + verbal noun
- Deferential expressions; vocative particles

1. Expressions with verb + verbal noun – general

In business, official and press Arabic, it is common to use a compound expression consisting of a *verb in a tense + a verbal noun* instead of a simple verb. We examine three important examples of this structure below; note that the meaning of the introductory verb is weakened, and it should not be interpreted or translated too literally.

2. قام يقوم ب *qāma yaqūmu bi-*

In B 17 we encountered the hollow verb قام يقوم ب I 'to undertake'. It is commonly used with a definite verbal noun (often in a construct) expressing the action:

قمنا بالجواب. *qumna bi-l-jawāb.*

('We undertook the reply') We replied.

سنقوم بافتتاح قنصلية. *sa-naqūm bi-ftitāḥ qunṣulīya.*

We shall open ('inaugurate') a consulate.

هل نقوم بالمفاوضة مع المتطرّفين؟ *(al-mutaṭarrifīn)*

Do we negotiate with extremists?

3. تمّ يتمّ *tamma yatimmu*

The doubled verb تمّ يتمّ I 'to (come to an) end' (B 14) is commonly used with a definite verbal noun (which may be one in construct) to denote an action in the passive (which may be an impersonal passive). By far the commonest use is in the *past tense* expressing a *completed* action, though the present is also found, relating to an ongoing action:

تمّ بناء سفارة جديدة. A new embassy was built.

تتمّ\تمّت دراسة المذكّرة. (*al-mudhakkara*)
The memorandum is being/was studied.
تمّ الوصول إلى اتّفاقية على ... Agreement was reached on ...

4. جرى يجري *jara yajrī*

The final-weak verb جرى يجري I 'to flow' in the meaning 'to proceed' (of discussions etc., B14) is also used in the present or past tense with a definite verbal noun (often in construct) expressing an *incomplete* action in the passive:

تجري دراسة التقرير الشفوي. (*at-taqrīr ash-shafawī*)
The note verbale is being studied.
جرى تحضير المذكّرة عندما... (*al-mudhakkara*)
The memorandum was being prepared when ...

5. Deferential expressions

It is important to know certain formal expressions of respect.

حضرة *ḥaḍra* **'presence'.** One use of this word is with a possessive suffix, 2nd or 3rd person. Its verb or adjective agrees with the person(s) indicated, not with the noun حضرة:

لو تفضّلت حضرتك *law tafaḍḍalt(i) ḥaḍratuka/ḥaḍratuki*
if you would be so kind
ماذا رجوا حضراتهم؟ *mādha rajaw ḥaḍrātuhum?*
What did they request?
حضرتها مريضة. (*ḥaḍratuha*) Madame is ill.

This is formal language; use it sparingly.

The following deferential expressions are very frequent in use. The verb and/or adjective agrees with the person:

حضرة *ḥaḍra* in the singular is also used in construct as part of a title:

حضرة السفير *ḥaḍrat as-safīr* Mr Ambassador
ماذا أمر حضرة الدكتور؟ What did the doctor order?

حضرة الوزير مريض. The minister is ill.

أستاذ *'ustādh* **'professor'**. This is used, by itself or in construct, for any person deemed to have erudition (in Italian, 'maestro'):

اتّصل الأستاذ محمود. *(maḥmūd)* (Mr) Mahmud rang.

حضرَت الأستاذة أيضًا. She (= an academic) also attended.

سيادة\سعادة *siyāda, sa'āda* **'excellency'**. These are used with a possessive suffix or in construct, in formal communication with or about someone senior. NB; the verb is always 3rd person:

كما تفضّل سيادة القاضي. *kama tafaḍḍal siyādat al-qāḍī.*
As His/Your Honour said ('was kind enough').

بشرط أنْ يوافق سعادة الرئيس *bi-sharṭ 'an yuwāfiq sa'ādat ar-ra'īs* provided/on condition that the President agrees

في حالة غيبة سيادته *fī ḥālat ghaybat siyādatihi*
in the case that H. E. is absent ('of H. E.'s absence')

6. Vocative particles

In addressing a person (even in writing) we often put a *vocative particle* before the name or title. The simplest such particle is يا *yā*, after which the name or title is in the definite form, but cannot begin with an article:

ما هو رأيك يا دكتور؟ What is your opinion, doctor?

يا سلام! ('O Peace!') Good heavens!

شكراً يا أحمد. *(shukran)* Thank you, Ahmad.

If the title is a construct, its theme stands in the *accusative* case:

يا مأموري القنصلية تفضّلوا معي. Consular officials ('Officials of the consulate'), please follow me.

A more formal particle is أيّها *'ayyuha* m. s./pl., أيّتها *'ayyatuha* f. s./pl., after which the title has the article, and is never in construct state:

أيّها المشاهدون\المستمعون الأعزاء ... *'ayyuha l-mushāhidūn/l-mustami'ūn al-'a'izzā'* ... Dear viewers/listeners ...

but: ... يا مشاهدي هذه النشرة ... Viewers of this bulletin ...

7. Vocabulary: الدبلوماسية *ad-diblomāsīya* Diplomacy

اعتماد (إلى)	*i'timād ('ila)* accreditation (to)
إكرامي	*'ikrāmī* courtesy (adj.)
امتياز	*imtiyāz* (also:) concession
انفرادي	*infirādī* unilateral
أوراق الاعتماد	*'awrāq al-i'timād* credentials
تأشيرة	*ta'shīra* annotation, (official language) visa
تشريفات	*tashrīfāt* (inan. pl.) protocol
توجه إلى	*tawajjaha* V *'ila* to turn towards
ثنائي	*thunā'ī* bilateral
جسوس جواسيس	*jasūs jawāsīs* spy
جسوسية	*jasūsīya* espionage
جنسية	*jinsīya* nationality
جهة	*jiha* side, direction, domain
عن جهتين	*'an jihatayn* bilaterally
عن جهة واحدة	*'an jiha wāḥida* unilaterally
جواز (سفر)	*jawāz (safar)* passport
حصانة	*ḥaṣāna* immunity
حفلة	*ḥafla* celebration, party
حكم ذاتي	*ḥukm dhātī* autonomy
خبر أخبار	*khabar 'akhbār* (also:) message
سر أسرار	*sirr 'asrār* secret (noun)
شفرة	*shifra* cypher, code
عزيز أعزاء	*'azīz 'a'izzā'* dear, beloved
فيزا\ڤيزا	*vīza* visa
قائم (قوام) بالأعمال	*qā'im* (pl. *quwwām*) *bi-l-'a'māl* chargé d'affaires
قنصل قناصل	*qunṣul qanāṣil* consul
لاجئ	*lāji'* refugee
لجوء	*lujū'* asylum

معتدل *mu'tádil* moderate
معتمد (إلى) *mu'támad ('ila)* accredited (to)
ملحق *mulḥaq* attaché
ملحق بحري\تجاري\ثقافي\للطيّران\عسكري
mulḥaq baḥrī/tijārī/thaqāfī/li-ṭ-ṭayyarān/'askarī
naval/commercial/cultural/air/military attaché

Exercise 1. Re-express with قام ب:

e.g.: أرسلوا خبراً شفريًا. ← قاموا بإرسال خبر شفري.
qāmū bi-'irsāl khabar shifrī.

١ سنجدّد البناية كلّها. ٢ سلّم الملحق تقريره السرّي.
٣ طبّقنا أنظمة القانون التجاري. ٤ يدرس السفير المذكّرة الآن.
٥ إنّهما افتتحا العلاقات الدبلوماسية.
٦ اتّخذنا هذه الإجراءات في مصالح اللاجئين.
٧ سيقدّم ناطق بلساننا اقتراحنا أمام الجلسة المقبلة.
٨ تصدر القنصلية الفيزات الإكرامية لكبار المأمورين فقط.

Exercise 2. Re-express with تمّ يتمّ or جرى يجري as appropriate:

e.g.: دُرست المذكّرة. ← تمّت دراسة للمذكّرة.
tammat dirāsat al-mudhakkara.
تُدرس المذكّرة. ← تجري دراسة المذكّرة.
tajrī dirāsat al-mudhakkara.

١ أُتّخذت الإجراءات المناسبة. ٢ طُبّقت نفس الأنظمة.
٣ تُبحث نفس الأنظمة. ٤ أُحتلّت المدينة كلّها.
٥ أُنسحب من المناطق المحتلّة. ٦ ووفق على البند الثالث.
٧ وُقّعت المذكّرة فوراً. ٨ متى ستُرسل المذكّرة؟

Exercise 3. Rewrite, using a deferential expression:

e.g.: هل سمع السفير عن هذا؟ ← هل سمع سيادة السفير عن هذا؟
hal sami' siyādat as-safīr 'an hādha?

هل سمعت (أنت) عن هذا ؟ ← هل سمعت حضرتك عن هذا ؟

hal sami't ḥaḍratuka/sami'ti ḥaḍratuki 'an hādha?

١ سيحضر الوزير الحفلة. ٢ لن يحضروا.
٣ نشكرك أيها القاضي. ٤ أين تسكن (هي) ؟
٥ أرجوك قلبيا يا معلّم. ٦ تفضّل بقبول هذا، يا مدير.

Exercise 4. Re-express without قام ب:

e.g.: *katab at-taqrīr.* كتب التقرير. ← قام بكتابة التقرير.

١ قمنا بشرح سياستنا. ٢ لم يقم بمفاوضة اي تعويض.
٣ سنقوم بالجواب على طلبهم. ٤ قام السفير بتقديم احتجاجنا.
٥ بعد دراسة قضية اللاجئين قمنا بمنح اللجوء.
٦ تقوم القنصلية بإصدار وتجديد جوازات السفر صباحا.

Exercise 5. Study this newspaper report:

وصل رئيس جنوب أفريقيا ثابو مبيكي *(thābu mbikī)* أمس إلى السودان في زيارة ستستغرق ثلاثة أيام سيجري خلالها محادثات(1) مع نظيره(2) السوداني عمر البشير*('umar al-bashīr)* حول السلام في البلاد. وسيتوجّه مبيكي خلال زيارته إلى منطقة دارفور*(dārfūr)* غرب السودان للاطّلاع على الوضع السائد(3) فيها بعد ٢٢ شهراً من الحرب الأهلية(4)، وسيشارك أيضاً في احتفال(5) بالذكرى(6) الـ٤٩ لاستقلال السودان الّذي يزوره للمرّة الأولى.

(from الحياة *Al-Hayat* newspaper, 31.12.2004)

(1) محادثة *muḥādatha* discussion
(2) نظير نظراء *naẓīr nuẓarā'* counterpart (3) سائد *sā'id* prevailing
(4) حرب أهلية *ḥarb 'ahlīya* civil war (5) احتفال *iḥtifāl* celebration
(6) ذكرى ذكريات *dhikra dhikrayāt* commemoration

Recount the story in your own words, covering at least these points:

١ أسماء المذكورين ووظيفتهما ٢ مدّة ومحلّ الزيارة
٣ برنامج الزائر ٤ الأزمة داخل السودان ٥ أساس الاحتفال

Exercise 6. Enlarge (125%) and fill in this UAE visa application:

بسم الله الرحمن الرحيم

دولة الإمارات العربية المتحدة

وزارة الداخليـــة

ادارة الجنسيـة والهجـــرة

الصورة
الشمسية

السفارة/القنصليـة في: ....

(طلب تأشيـرة زيـارة)

بيـانات مقدّم الطلب:

الاسم الكامل: .... اسم الأب: .... اسم الأم: ....

الجنسية: .... محل الولادة: .... تاريخ الولادة: ....

المهنة: .... رقم الجواز: .... نوع الجواز (عادي/وثيقة سفر) ....

محلّ الإصدار: .... تاريخ الإصدار: .... تاريخ الانتهاء: ....

(الأشخاص المرافقيـن)

الاسم الصلة

١) ....

٢) ....

٣) ....

العنوان الدائم: ....

الغرض من الزيارة: ....

صلة ما بين الكفيل والمكفول: ....

التاريخ: ....

توقيع مقدّم الطلب

....

بيـانات الكفيـل:

الاسم الكامل: .... الجنسية: ....

المهنة: .... جهة العمل: ....

الإمارة: .... هاتف العمل: ....

عنوان السكن: .... المنطقة: ....

الشارع: .... رقم هاتف المنزل: ....

أتعهّد بأن أكون مسؤولاً عن ضمان صحّة المعلومات المدوّنة في هذا الطلب وعن التزام المكفول بالأنظمة المرعية في البلاد وتأمين نفقات تسفيرة عند الإقتضاء.

التاريخ: ....

توقيع الكفيل

....

(للاستعمال الرسمي)

رأي السفارة/القنصلية	موافقة إدارة الجنسية والهجرة

(copied by permission of the Ministry of the Interior, Abu Dhabi)

بسم الله الرحمن الرحيم *bi-sm illāh ar-raḥmān ar-raḥīm* in the name of God, the Merciful, the Compassionate

دولة الإمارات العربية المتّحدة دولة الامارات العربية المتحدة

صورة شمسية *ṣūra shamsīya* (official language) photograph

رافق *rāfaqa* III to accompany

صلة *ṣila* connexion

كفيل كفلاء *kafīl kufalā'* sponsor

كفل يكفل *kafala yakfulu* I to sponsor, to secure

هاتف هواتف *hātif hawātif* (official language) telephone

تعهّد *ta'ahhada* V to commit oneself

صحّة *ṣiḥḥa* (here:) correctness

دوّن *dawwana* II to place on record

التزم *iltázama* VIII to be obliged

مرعيّ *mar'īy* complied with

نفقة *nafaqa* expense

سفّر *saffara* II to send (a person)

اقتضى *iqtáḍa* VIII to necessitate

Exercise 7. Re-express with a passive verb:

e.g. تم ارسال جواب الحكومة. ← أرسل جواب الحكومة.

'ursil jawāb al-ḥukūma.

١ جرى بحث الشروط يومين. ٢ تم نشر نص منح الحصانة.

٣ تم الوصول الى وضع مشترك بين الطرفين.

٤ تم استلام خبر سري وشفري. ٥ يجري تحضير نص البنود.

٦ تم منح الحكم الذاتي بعد مفاوضات ثنائية طويلة وصعبة.

11 Structures – 3

- Improper agreement
- Case endings

1. Improper agreement

Examine these expressions:

سياسيون كبار القوة *siyāsīyūn kibār al-quwa*
politicians of great power ('great the power')

في حركة واسعة النفوذ *fī ḥaraka wāsi'a n-nufūdh*
in a movement with wide influence

لناس ضعفاء الفهم *li-nās ḍu'afā' al-fahm*
to/for people with poor ('weak') understanding

ردّ فعل شديد اللهجة *radd fi'l shadīd al-lahja*
a strongly worded reaction ('strong the accent')

Here, a noun and adjective (underlined) are combined in the 'wrong' order to make a compound adjective; and the adjective element of the compound is made to agree grammatically with the 'wrong' noun, i.e. :

كبار with سياسيون (m. pl.) and not with القوة (f. sing.),
واسعة with حركة (f. sing.) and not with النفوذ (m. sing.),
ضعفاء with الناس (m. pl.) and not with الفهم (m. sing.).
شديد with ردّ فعل (m. sing.) and not with اللهجة (f. sing.)

These examples are indefinite, since the noun described by the compound is indefinite. To make the whole expression definite, make all its components definite:

السياسيون الكبار القوة the politicians of great power
في الحركة الواسعة النفوذ in the movement with wide influence
للناس الضعفاء الفهم to/for the people with poor understanding
ردّ الفعل الشديد اللهجة the strongly worded reaction

This structure is called *improper agreement* (الإضافة غير الحقيقية *al-'iḍāfa ghayr al-ḥaqīqīya*).

The same meanings can also be expressed in other ways:

- with ذو\ذات (etc., B 24), in indefinite or definite construct:
  في (الـ)حركة ذات (الـ)نفوذ (الـ)واسع *fī ḥaraka dhāt nufūdh wāsiʿ/fi l-ḥaraka dhāt an-nufūdh al-wāsiʿ*
- with an indefinite or definite relative clause (B 35):
  مع (الـ)سياسيين (الّذين) لهم قوة كبيرة
  maʿ (as-)siyāsīyīn (alladhīna) lahum quwa kabīra
- with a preposition: ناس بفهم ضعيف\ناس بالفهم الضعيف
  nās bi-fahm ḍaʿīf/nās bi-l-fahm aḍ-ḍaʿīf

In all these alternative structures any agreement is of course 'proper'.

2. Case endings

In B 10 we encountered the full pronunciation of the noun case-ending in some expressions with السنة:

في السنة الماضية\الجارية *fi s-sanati l-māḍiya/l-jāriya*

We have this phenomenon in a few other set expressions. Note:

العربية السعودية *al-ʿarabīyatu s-saʿūdīya*

في العربية السعودية *fi l-ʿarabīyati s-saʿūdīya*

لا بدّ من (أنّ) *lā budda min* + verbal noun or *'anna* (see B 23) one cannot escape/avoid

لا بدّ من احتياج إلى الإصلاح. *(al-'iṣlāḥ)* We cannot escape the need for reform.
لا بدّ من أنّنا نحتاج إلى الإصلاح.

من جهة *min jihatin* on (the) one hand

من جهة أخرى *min jihatin 'ukhra* on the other hand

شخص ما *shakhṣun mā* somebody or other

لأمر ما *li-'amrin mā* for some reason

بطريقة ما *bi-ṭarīqatin mā* somehow

Note also: نوعا ما *nawʿan mā* somewhat

كثيراً ما\قليلاً ما *kathīran mā/qalīlan mā* often/seldom

يوما ما *yawman mā* one of these days

3. Vocabulary: التاريخ *at-tārīkh* **History**

أصلح	*'aṣlaḥa* IV to reform
ألغى	*'algha* IV to cancel, abolish
أمير أمراء	*'amīr 'umarā'* prince, emir
انفصل (عن)	*infáṣala* VII *('an)* to separate, secede (from)
ثورة	*thawra* revolution
حرر	*ḥarrara* II to liberate, emancipate
حرب عالمية	*ḥarb 'ālamīya* world war
حلف	*ḥilf* alliance
حليف حلفاء	*ḥalīf ḥulafā'* ally
حياد	*ḥiyād* neutrality
دين أديان	*dīn 'adyān* religion
ذاتي	*dhātī* autonomous
راديكالي	*rādīkālī* radical
رجعي	*raj'ī* reactionary
ردّ (ردود) فعل (على)	*radd* (pl. *rudūd) fi'l ('ala)* reaction (to)
زعيم زعماء	*za'īm zu'amā'* leader
شأن شؤون	*sha'n shu'ūn* matter
شعب شعوب	*sha'b shu'ūb* people
شيوعي	*shuyū'ī* communist
صهيوني	*ṣahyūnī* Zionist
صوّت (ل\ضدّ)	*ṣawwata* II *(li-, ḍidd)* to vote (for/against)
طريقة طرائق	*ṭarīqa ṭarā'iq* way, manner
ظالم ظلاّم	*ẓālim ẓullām* tyrant, oppressive
ظلم يظلم	*ẓalama yaẓlimu* I to oppress
ظلم	*ẓulm* oppression
عدوّ أعداء	*'adūw 'a'dā'* enemy
عصر عصور	*'aṣr 'uṣūr* age, era
العصور\القرون الوسطى	*al-'uṣūr/al-qurūn al-wusṭa* the Middle Ages

قاوم *qāwama* III to resist
قرن قرون *qarn qurūn* century
مطلق *muṭlaq* absolute
ملك ملوك\ملكة *malik mulūk* king; *malika* queen
منظّمة التحرير الفلسطينية *munaẓẓamat at-taḥrīr al-filasṭīnīya* Palestine Liberation Organisation, PLO
نهاية *nihāya* end
نهايةً\في النهاية *nihāyatan, fi n-nihāya* finally
هدّد (ب) *haddada* II *(bi-)* to threaten (with)

Exercise 1. Make an indefinite expression with improper agreement:

e.g.: مصرف (أموال محدودة) ← مصرف محدود الأموال

maṣrif maḥdūd al-'amwāl

١ زعيم (سياسة رجعية) ٢ زعماء (سياسات رجعية)
٣ اسم ملك (سلطة مطلقة) ٤ في ثورة (أساس شعبي)
٥ نائب شيوعي (أفكار رادكالية) ٦ مدّة (تغييرات كبيرة)
٧ قرن (تغييرات كبيرة) ٨ قرون (تغييرات كبيرة)
٩ إجراء (نتيجة إيجابية) ١٠ اتّخاذ إجراء (نتيجة إيجابية)

Now make all your answers definite:

e.g. المصرف (أموال محدودة) ← المصرف المحدود الأموال

al-maṣrif al-maḥdūd al-'amwāl

Exercise 2. Recast your answers to Exercise 1 using ذو (etc.):

e.g.: مصرف محدود الأموال ← مصرف ذو أموال محدودة

maṣrif dhū 'amwāl maḥdūda

المصرف المحدود الأموال ← المصرف ذو الأموال المحدودة

al-maṣrif dhu l-'amwāl al-maḥdūda

Exercise 3. Rewrite, using an expression with improper agreement:

e.g.: حركة لها برنامج غال ← حركة غالية البرنامج

ḥaraka ghāliya l-barnāmaj

الحركة ذات البرنامج الغالي ← الحركة الغالية البرنامج

al-ḥaraka l-ghāliya l-barnāmaj

١ الحركة الّتي لها برنامج غال ٢ حركة مقاومة بأعضاء أقلاّء

٣ بضائع لأسعار مرتفعة ٤ ثورة نجحت نجاحًا تامّاً

٥ الزعماء الّذين عندهم غرض واضح ٦ شعب ذو تاريخ طويل

٧ قوة الناس ذوي المال الكثير ٨ طلمبة بقوة كبيرة

Exercise 4. Expand or complete sentences 1 to 6 with expressions 7 to 12, giving any alternatives possible:

e.g.: نستمرّ في الإصلاحات | لا بدّ من

لا بدّ من أنّا نستمرّ في الإصلاحات

lā budda min 'anna nastamirr fī l-'iṣlāḥāt.

١ كانت ثورة اجتماعية ضرورية.	٧ لا بدّ من
٢ إنّ الثورة الاجتماعية ضرورية.	٨ لأمر ما
٣ اتّصل ...، لا نعرف من.	٩ كثيراً ما
٤ يفضلون أن يشتغلوا بالإنجليزية.	١٠ نوعًا ما
٥ فشل الانقلاب.	١١ من جهة أخرى
٦ محاولة ثانية لإصلاح المجلس.	١٢ بشخص ما

Exercise 5. Complete each sentence with your own words:

e.g.: فشل اقتراح الإصلاح لأنّ ... ← ... لأنّ المعارضة رفضته.

fashil iqtirāḥ al-'iṣlāḥ li'anna l-mu'āraḍa rafaḍat-hu.

١ فشل اقتراح الإصلاح بسبب ...

٢ بعد الحرب العالمية الأولى ...

٣ بعد الحرب العالمية الثانية ...

٤ قبل تأسيس إسرائيل كانت القدس ...

٥ الفرق بين الرجعية والراديكالية هو ...

٦ صوت الاشتراكيون ضدّ الاقتراح ...

٧ أساس الصهيونية هو ...

٨ ... إنشاء دولة فلسطينية حرّة ومستقلّة.

٩ أديان الشرق الأوسط الرئيسية هي ...

١٠ إن إنشاء السلام الدائم في الشرق الأوسط يتوقّف على ...

Exercise 6. Study this text about the Kurds, deducing for yourself the meaning of the words marked '†'. Then answer the questions:

كردستان† والانفصال ... تهديدات لن تتمّ!
حقّقوا† نظامهم الذاتي وسيظلّون عراقيين

ما الّذي يحدث في كردستان؟ لقد كنت دومًا(1) متعاطفًا(2) مع الأكراد† وأدعو(3) إلى أحقّيتهم(4) في دولة كردية تضمّ أكراد تركيا† ١٤ مليونًا، وإيران† ٧ ملايين، ومليونين بكردستان العراق وهذه الدعوة(5) قد تستحيل(6) في الزمن(7) المنظور(8) بسبب تركيا ثمّ(9) إيران بل(10) تهدّد تركيا بالحرب لمنع تحقيقها لكنّ العالم أجمع(11) والعرب والمسلمين يعرفون ومطّلعون(12) على أن كردستان العراق تحظى(13) بامتيازات كالعراقيين في جميع شؤون حياتهم وهو ما لا يتوفّر(14) لإخوانهم في تركيا وإيران ...

(from العرب/*Al-Arab* newspaper, 9.2.05)

(1) دومًا *dawman* constantly

(2) متعاطف مع *muta'āṭif ma'* sympathetic to

(3) دعا يدعو إلى *da'a yad'ū* I *'ila* to call for

(4) أحقّية في *'aḥaqqīya fī* rightful claim to

(5) دعوة *da'wa* call

(6) استحال *istaḥāla* X to be unthinkable

(7) زمن أزمان *zaman 'azmān* time

(8) منظور *manẓūr* foreseeable

(9) ثمّ *thumma* and then

(10) بل *bal* but rather

(11) أجمع *'ajma'* the entire

(12) مطّلع على *muṭṭáli' 'ala* aware of

(13) حظي يحظى ب *ḥáẓiya yaḥẓa* I *bi-* to enjoy

(14) توفّر *tawaffara* V to abound

١ أين تسكن أكثرية الأكراد؟ وأين أصغر عدد منهم؟
٢ من الّذي يعارض أشدّ المعارضة فكرة استقلال الأكراد؟
٣ اشرح الفرق بين حياة الأكراد العراقيين ووضع الأكراد الآخرين.
٤ أيّة أقلّيات أخرى تسكن في العراق؟

12 Structures – 4

- Expressions of circumstance
- re-

1. Expressions of circumstance – general

Expressions of circumstance (حال أحوال *ḥāl 'aḥwāl*) show an action or state accompanying the verb on which they depend. There are three common types of such expression: the *accusative* of circumstance, the *verb* of circumstance and the *clause* of circumstance.

2. Accusative of circumstance

The accompanying action or state can be expressed with the indefinite accusative of the appropriate noun or adjective (most often in the form of an active participle). Some examples of this kind resemble one of the accusative uses studied in Chapter 9:

عرفناه مساعداً فنّياً. *'arafnāhu musā'idan fannīyan.*
We knew him as a technical assistant.

ترك البلاد فقيراً ورجع غنياً. *(faqīran ... ghanīyan)*
He left the country poor and returned rich.

وصلوا متأخّرين. *(muta'akhkhirīn)* They arrived late.

أضاف المختار قائلاً ... *(qā'ilan)* The mayor added ...
('said, adding ...')

احتجّوا مشيرين إلى الأرقام. *(mushīrin 'ila)* They protested, referring to the figures.

اتّصلت الوكالة مقدّمةً عون الطوارئ. *(muqaddimatan 'awn aṭ-ṭawāri')* The agency telephoned offering emergency aid.

3. Verb of circumstance

The accompanying action or state can also be expressed with a verb with the same subject as the main verb. The verb of circumstance is always in the present tense, irrespective of the tense of the main verb:

أضاف المختار يقول ... *(yaqūl)* The mayor added ...

احتخّوا يشيرون إلى الأرقام. *(yushīruna 'ila)* They protested, referring to the figures.

وزّعنا الغذاء نستعمل شاحنات وكالة العون.

wazza'na l-ghidhā' nastá'mil shāḥināt wikālat al-'awn.

We distributed the food using the aid agency lorries.

جاوبوا فوراً يلغون الدين. *(yulghūna)*

They responded immediately, cancelling the debt.

اتّصلت الوكالة تقدّم عون الطوارئ. *(tuqaddim al-'awn aṭ-ṭawāri')*

The agency telephoned offering emergency aid.

4. Clause of circumstance

We can also use a clause to express the accompanying action or state. In a circumstantial clause:

- the subject may be different from that of the other clause,
- the circumstantial clause is introduced by و *wa-*, which then expresses time ('as', 'when', 'while' B 36) or condition or concession ('if (not)', 'whereas', 'while' (B 37); see also below,
- the verb is mostly present in tense (or the clause is an equation),
- و is followed immediately by one of the following:
  - the subject (noun or *stated* pronoun) of the clause,
  - قد + past tense (for an earlier action; the قد is never omitted),
  - a negative particle or ليس (etc.).

نوينا مراجعة المشروع وهو يريد تمديده. *nawayna murāja'at al-mashrū' wa-huwa yurīd tamdīdahu.* We intended to revise the project, while/whereas he wanted to extend it.

إنّا تردّدنا أن نستثمر أكثر والأسعار مرتفعة.

'inna taraddadna 'an nastathmir 'akthar wa-l-'as'ār murtáfi'a.

We hesitated to invest more while prices were ('are') high.

لا يمكنهم أن يستمرّوا ولا يضمن البنك تكاليف التشغيل.

(wa-lā yaḍman al-bank takālīf at-tashghīl) They cannot continue if the bank does not guarantee the operating costs.

Some circumstantial clauses translate into English as a non-identifying relative expression with 'which' or 'who'. (A non-identifying relative does not identify the antecedent (B 35), it merely adds information about it. Arabic does not use a relative expression at all here.):

قدّموا قرضًا تجاريًا قصيراً الأجل وهذا أشدّ نوع من العون.
qaddamū qarḍan tijārīyan qaṣīran al-'ajal wa-hādha 'ashadd naw' min al-'awn. They offered a short-term commercial loan, which is ('and that is') the hardest form of aid.

يجب أن نبحث عقد التمويل وفيه مشكلتان. We have to discuss the financing contract, in which ('and in it') there are two problems.

The circumstantial clause may interrupt the main clause:

مندوب الصندوق وهو مهندس مدني يتركّز في مشاريع رأسمالية.
mandūb aṣ-ṣandūq wa-huwa muhandis madanī yatarakkaz fī mashārī' ra'smālīya. The Fund delegate, who is a civil engineer, concentrates on capital projects.

5. re-

The meaning 'again' can be expressed in Arabic with the verb أعاد *'a'āda* IV 'to do again'. It is followed by a definite verbal noun (which may be in construct):

أعدنا تقدير المشروع. *'a'adna taqdīr al-mashrū'.* We re-estimated the project.

Its verbal noun إعادة *'i'āda* is used as often as the verbal form:

تمّت إعادة تحرير النصّ. *tammat 'i'ādat taḥrīr an-naṣṣ.*
(See Chapter 10) The text has been re-edited.

so also, e.g.: إعادة التوزيع *'i'ādat at-tawzī'* redistribution
إعادة الحساب *'i'ādat al-ḥisāb* recalculation

Remember to drop the article from the theme of a construct:

إعادة حساب الدين *'i'ādat ḥisāb ad-dayn* recalculation of the debt

Do not confuse this Form IV verb with its Form I counterpart (عاد يعود, B 18), which has similar meaning but behaves differently.

6. Vocabulary: العون للتنمية *al-ʿawn li-t-tánmiya*
Development aid

أجل آجال *'ajal 'ājāl* term, deadline
أسّس *'assasa* II to establish
اقترض (من) *iqtárada* VIII *(min)* to borrow (from)
أقرض *'aqrada* IV to lend to
على الأقلّ *ʿala l-'aqall* at least
أوّلي *'awwalī* primary, basic
إعادة البناء *'iʿādat al-binā'* reconstruction
إعادة الإنشاء *'iʿādat al-'inshā'* restructuring
برنامج الأمم المتّحدة الإنمائي *barnāmaj al-'umam al-muttáḥida l-'inmā'ī* United Nations Development Program, UNDP
بنية تحتية *binya taḥtīya* infrastructure
تدريب أثناء العمل *tadrīb 'athnā' al-ʿamal* on-the-job training
حالة الطوارئ *ḥālat aṭ-ṭawāri'* state of emergency
خرج *kharj* expenditure
دعم *daʿm* support
راجع *rājaʿa* III to review, to revise
سدّد *saddada* II to repay
صندوق النقد الدولي *ṣandūq an-naqd ad-duwali* International Monetary Fund, IMF
صنّع *ṣannaʿa* II to industrialise
ضمان *ḍamān* guarantee
ضمن يضمن *ḍamina yaḍmanu* I to guarantee
طرئة طوارئ *ṭari'a ṭawari'* emergency
عضوية *ʿuḍwīya* membership
مدّد *maddada* II to extend (something)
مساواة *musāwā* equality
مؤسّسة *mu'assasa* foundation
نفّذ *naffadha* II to implement

نهائي *nihā'ī* final
هدف أهداف *hadaf 'ahdāf* goal
نوّع *nawwa'a* II to diversify
وزّع *wazza'a* II to distribute

Exercise 1. Join as one sentence, using an accusative of circumstance:
e.g.: شرح الخطّة. ذكر دور البنك. ← شرح الخطّة ذاكراً دور البنك.
sharaḥ al-khiṭṭa dhākiran dawr al-bank.

١ رفضت اللجنة الضمان المقترح. راجعت جميع الشروط.
٢ غيّروا شروط القرض. خفّضوا الفائدة السنوية بـ ٥،٠٪.
٣ ساعدت الحكومة الجديدة اقتصاد البلاد. أيّدت القطاع الخاصّ.
٤ يلعب البنك دوراً هامّاً. يقدّم قروض واطئة الفائدة للفلّاحين.
٥ ترك الوفد البلاد. رجع إلى باريس.

Exercise 2. Join as one sentence, using a verb of circumstance:
e.g.: شرح الخطّة. ذكر دور البنك. ← شرح الخطّة يذكر دور البنك.
sharaḥ al-khiṭṭa yadhkur dawr al-bank.

١ خفّضنا الخرج. تركّزنا في التدريب أثناء العمل.
٢ أعلنت الحكومة حالة الطوارئ. طلب العون الدولي.
٣ أعدنا تخطيط قطاع النقل. مددنا البنية التحتية المتعلّقة به.
٤ نؤيّد تصنيع البلاد. زدنا الضرائب على المستوردات.
٥ بدأوا البحث. سألوا رأينا بخصوص تنفيذ العون الغذائي.

Exercise 3. Join as one sentence, using a clause of circumstance:
e.g.: شرح الخطة. الأرقام معقدة. ← شرح الخطّة والأرقام معقّدة.
sharaḥ al-khiṭṭa wa-l-'arqām mu'aqqada.

١ سأل الرئيس الخبراء. الرئيس ليس مؤهلا في الاقتصاد.
٢ كيف يمكننا ان نفاوض؟ ليست عندنا بضائع قابلة للبيع.
٣ لا نستطيع قبول قروض جديدة. ان وضع اقتصادنا ضعيف.
٤ اعدنا انجاز المشروع. انحلت المشاكل المالية.
٥ قاموا بإنجاز البرنامج. كانوا على علم بعدم استقرار القطاع.

Exercise 4. Repeat Exercises 1 to 3, giving your own expression of circumstance (of any kind) for each sentence:

e.g.: شرح الخطّة متركّزاً في تفاصيل التنفيذ.

sharah al-khitta mutarakkizan fī tafāṣīl at-tanfīdh.

شرح الخطّة يتركّز في تفاصيل التنفيذ.

sharah al-khitta yatarakkaz fī tafāṣīl at-tanfīdh.

شرح الخطّة ونحن كنّا نشكّ في إفادتها.

sharah al-khitta wa-naḥnu kunna nashukk fī 'ifādatiha.

Exercise 5. Express a repeated action, using a form of أعاد IV:

e.g.: *'a'ādū sharḥ al-khiṭṭa.* شرحوا الجطّة. ← أعادوا شرح الخطّة.

'i'ādat taqdīr al-khiṭṭa تقدير الجطّة ← إعاة تقدير الخطّة

١ استكشاف المنطقة   ٢ استكشفوا المنطقة.

٣ أنجزنا المشاريع الريفية.   ٤ توزيع العون الغذائي

٥ استأجرنا شاحنات الوكالة.   ٦ ذكروا الموضوع.

٧ إنشاء اقتصاد البلاد   ٨ ذِكر الموضوع

Exercise 6. Recast the sentence with an expression of circumstance:

e.g.: كان الوضع صعباً عندما اتّصلنا بالسلطات.

← كان الوضع صعباً ونحن نتّصل بالسلطات.

kān al-waḍ' ṣa'ban wa-naḥnu nattásil bi-s-sulṭāt .

١ لا نستطيع المساعدة إذا لم توافق السلطات المحلّية.

٢ كتبوا تقريراً اقترحوا فيه مراجعة البنية التحتية كلّها .

٣ لا تنجح جهود السكّان إلاّ إذا ساعدهم الصندوق.

٤ اقترضنا مبلغاً كبيراً ضمنّا تسديده تحت شروط طويلة الأجل.

٥ وقعنا العقد بينما هو طلب نسخةً من أجل مديره.

Exercise 7. Recast the sentence without an expression of circumstance:

e.g.: غيّروا الاقتراح يضيفون شروطًا أشدّ إلينا .

← غيّروا الاقتراح بإضافة شروط أشدّ إلينا .

ghayyaru l-iqtirāḥ bi-'iḍāfat shurūṭ 'ashadd 'ilayna .

١ اقترحوا شروطًا ونحن نرفضها بعد استشار خبرائنا.
٢ ساعدنا البنك الدولي ممدداً قروضنا الثلاثة الطويلة الأجل.
٣ تحاول الحكومة تجديد الاقتصاد متركّزةً في إعادة إنشاء قطاع الصادرات.
٤ نفضّل التدريب أثناء العمل وهو أسهل وأرخص وأسرع.
٥ أيّدهم البنك يمنحهم قرضًا خاصاً منخفضًا الفائدة.

Exercise 8. Study this text about the Arab Bank for Economic Development in Africa (BADEA), deducing the meaning of the words marked '†'. Then answer the questions:

تعريف(1) بالمصرف

تأسّس† المصرف العربي للتنمية الاقتصادية في أفريقيا بمقتضى(2) قرار من مؤتمر القمّة العربي السادس المنعقد بالجزائر ٢٨ نوفمبر ١٩٧٣، وبدأ عمليته في مارس ١٩٧٥. واتّخذ من(3) الخرطوم عاصمة جمهورية السودان مقراً(4) له.

المصرف مؤسّسة مالية تموّلها حكومات الدول الإعضاء بجامعة الدول العربية الموقّعة على اتّفاقية إنشائه في ١٨ فبراير ١٩٧٤. وهو مؤسّسة دولية مستقلّة، يتمتّع(5) بالشخصية† القانونية الدولية الكاملة، وبالاستقلال التامّ في المجالين(6) الإداري والمالي، ويخضع(7) لأحكام اتفاقية إنشائه ومبادئ القانون الدولي.

يُعدّ† إنشاء المصرف استجابةً† لهدف دعم التعاون الاقتصادي والمالي بين المنطقتين العربية والأفريقية وتجسيداً(8) للتضامن† العربي الأفريقي، وترسيخاً(9) لمشروع التعاون على أسس من المساواة والصداقة†. وتحقيقًا لهذا الهدف، عُهد(10) إلى المصرف بمهمّة:

- الإسهام† في تمويل التنمية في الدول الأفريقية غير العربية.
- تشجيع مشاركة رؤوس الأموال العربية في التنمية الأفريقية.
- الإسهام في توفير(11) المعونة(12) الفنّية اللازمة(13) للتنمية في أفريقيا.

(official definition of المصرف العربي للتنمية الاقتصادية في أفريقيا BADEA, reproduced by permission of the Bank)

(1) تعريف ب *ta'rīf bi-* definition of

(2) بمقتضى *bi-muqtaḍa* in conformity with

(3) اتّخذ من *ittákhadha* VIII *min* to make (something) into (something)

(4) مقرّ مقارّ *maqarr maqārr* headquarters

(5) تمتّع ب *tamatta'a* V *bi-* to enjoy (6) مجال *majāl* domain, range

(7) بخضع ل *bi-khuḍu' li-* governed by (8) تجسيد *tajsīd* embodiment

(9) ترسيخ *tarsīkh* securing

(10) عهد يعهد إلى ب *'ahida ya'hadu* I *'ila* (pers.) *bi-* (thg.) to entrust

(11) توفير *tawfīr* provision (12) معونة *ma'ūna* assistance

(13) لازم *lāzim* necessary

١ متى وكيف أنشئ المصرف؟ ٢ اشرح وضعه القانوني.
٣ له ثلاثة أهداف. ما هي؟ ٤ في أيّة بلدان يعمل المصرف؟
٥ ما هو أساس علاقة المصرف مع البلدان المستفيدة من عونه ؟

Now show how you deduced the meaning of each word marked '†'.

13 Structures – 5

- Topic and comment
- Proposals and wishes

1. Topic and comment

Examine two sentences with the same meaning but different emphasis:

تقرّر الصحافة الطقس كلّ يوم. *tuqarrir aṣ-ṣiḥāfa ṭ-ṭaqs kull yawm.*
The press reports the weather every day.

الطقس تقرّره الصحافة كلّ يوم. *aṭ-ṭaqs, tuqarriruhu ṣ-ṣiḥāfa kull yawm.*('The weather, the press reports it every day.')
The weather is reported by the press every day./
The weather is something the press reports every day.

The first variant is in the standard style which we have studied.

In the second, the direct object leads the sentence for emphasis. It is followed by a slight pause in reading, and is reiterated with an object suffix on the verb (as in relative clauses, B 35). The object must be *definite* in this structure.

We can call this device *Topic and Comment* (Arabic جملة ذات وجهين *jumla dhāt wajhayn*: جملة جمل *jumla jumal* 'sentence', وجه وجوه *wajh wujūh* 'face'). The object is the topic, the rest of the sentence is the comment on it.

In English we often have to use a passive to get the desired word-order and emphasis: 'The weather *is reported* by the press ...'. Using topic and comment in Arabic avoids the passive, and is good style.

Topic and comment can be used also for a prepositional object (in which case the object is reiterated as a suffix on its preposition):

الرطوبة يتكلّم الجميع عنها. *ar-ruṭūba, yatakallam al-jamīʻ ʻanha.* Everyone is talking about the humidity.

For a construct, we can advance the whole construct, or its attribute alone. Whatever is advanced must be appropriately reiterated, with an object suffix or a possessive sufffix:

استكشاف الفضاء، لم يفهمه أحد. *istikshāf al-faḍā', lam yafhamhu 'aḥad.* Nobody understood space exploration.

الفضاء، لم يفهم أحد طبيعته. *al-faḍā', lam yafham 'aḥad ṭabī'atahu.* Nobody understood the nature of space.

The topic-and-comment does not affect the verbal-sentence structure:

أمطار الخريف ينتظرها القرويون. *'amṭār al-kharīf, yantaẓiruha l-qarawīyūn.* The villagers are waiting for the autumn rains.

See the last Arabic example in B 15, para. 3, for a similar structure.

2. Proposals and wishes

Proposals. Proposals for action to be taken by the first or third persons ('let me/us/him/her/it/them...' are expressed with ل *li- + jussive* (B 23):

لنسأله. *li-nas'alhu.* Let us ask him.

ليدخل. *li-yadkhul.* Let/Have him come in.

Stronger variants of ل *li-* are فل *fa-l-*, ول *wa-l-* 'so/'then let ...'

فليقدّموا طلبهم. *fa-l-yuqaddimū ṭalabahum.* So let them make ('advance') their claim./Let them make their claim, then.

Note that ل loses its own vowel in these compounds.

This structure is the nearest equivalent to an *affirmative imperative* (see B 25) for the first and third persons.

For negative proposals, the negative imperative structure (لا + jussive) is used equally for all three persons:

لا تنتظر\تنتظري\تنتظروا. Do not wait.

لا ننتظر\ينتظروا. Let us/them not wait.

Similary, *indirect command* (B 33), both affirmative and negative, can apply to all three persons:

أرجوك أن تسمع.\أرجوه أن يسمع. I ask you/him to listen.

طلبنا ألاّ تخرجوا\يخرجوا. We asked you/them not to leave.

Wishes. The simplest way to express a wish is as an unreal condition (B 37), usually with no stated response:

لو كان يوم الجمعة! If (only) it were Friday!

لو لم يعملوا هكذا. I wish they would not do (like) that.

لو تفضّلتم بالجواب If you would be so good as to reply

and, already studied: لو سمحت Please ('If you would permit.')

3. Vocabulary: الجغرافية والمناخ والفضاء

al-jughrāfīya wa-l-munākh wa-l-faḍā'

Geography, climate, space

أطلق *'aṭlaqa* IV to fire

البحر الأبيض (المتوسّط) *al-baḥr al-'abyaḍ (al-mutawassiṭ)* Mediterranean Sea

البحر الأحمر *al-baḥr al-'aḥmar* Red Sea

بحيرة بحائر *buḥayra baḥā'ir* lake

برد *bard* cold(ness)

تثلج السماء *tathluj as-samā'* it is snowing

تثلّج *tathallaja* V to become frozen

تمطر السماء *tamṭur as-samā'* it is raining

ثلج ثلوج *thalj thulūj* snow

جغرافية *jughrāfīya* geography

حارّ *ḥārr* hot

دجلة *dijla* Tigris

دلتا *dilta* delta

دنيا *dunya* world

رطب *raṭb* humid

رطوبة *ruṭūba* humidity

ريح رياح *rīḥ riyāḥ* (f.) wind

سحاب *saḥāb* clouds

سحابة سحب *saḥāba suḥub* cloud

سفينة الفضاء *safīnat al-faḍā'* spaceship

سماء سماوات *samā' samāwāt* (m./f.) sky

الشرق الأقصى *ash-sharq al-'aqṣa* Far East

شمس شموس *shams shumūs* (f.) sun

صاروخ صواريخ *ṣārūkh ṣawārīkh* rocket
طبيعة *ṭabī'a* nature
طقس *ṭaqs* weather
طيران\رحلة في الفضاء *ṭayarān/riḥla fī l-faḍā'* space flight
عظيم عظماء *'aẓīm 'uẓamā'* huge; splendid
الفرات *al-furāt* Euphrates
فضاء *faḍā'* space
فضائي *faḍā'ī* space traveller, cosmonaut
قمر أقمار *qamar 'aqmār* moon
قمر صناعي *qamar ṣinā'ī* satellite
كوكب كواكب *kawkab kawākib* planet
المحيط الأطلسي\الأطلنطي *al- muḥīṭ al-'aṭlasī/al-'aṭlanṭī* Atlantic Ocean
المحيط الهادي\الهندي *al-muḥīṭ al-hādī/al-hindī* Pacific/Indian Ocean
مطر أمطار *maṭar 'amṭār* rain
مضيق مضايق *maḍīq maḍāyiq* strait
مناخ *munākh* climate
ناشف *nāshif* dry
نجم نجوم *najm nujūm* star
نشف *nashaf* dryness
واد\الوادي وديان *wādin, al-wādī* (weak) *widyān* valley

Exercise 1. Recast the sentence as topic and comment:

e.g.: يهتمّ الفلاّحون بالمطر اهتمامًا كبيراً.

← المطر يهتمّ البفلاّحون به اهتمامًا كبيراً.

al-matar, yahtimm al-fallāḥun bihi htimāman kabīran.

١ لا يستغرب أحد من استكشاف الفضاء في الوقت الحاضر.

٢ قد كتب كتّاب مختلفون عن النيل العظيم.

٣ لا يخاف الأطفال أبداً من الثلج.

٤ لا يخافون الثلج أبداً ويلعبون فيه.
٥ هل يعرف مديرك تركيا وإيران؟
٦ قد أرسل الأمريكيون أكبر صاروخ إلى القمر أمس.
٧ قرأنا جميعنا عن البحر الأحمر في دراستنا للتاريخ القديم.
٨ كان الطقس رطباً جداً ولم نرى الشمس إلاّ قليلاً.
٩ إنّا لا نفهم جيداً الوضع السياسي في الشرق الأقصى.
١٠ لا يعرف أحد عدد الأقمار الصناعية الدائرة حول الدنيا حاليًا.

Exercise 2. Using the verb quoted, make a proposal for action by (a) نحن (b) هي , (c) هم:

e.g.: ذهب ← لنذهب، لتذهب، ليذهبوا

li-nadhhab, li-tadhhab, li-yadhhabū

١ اتّصل فيهم	٢ جاوب	٣ انتظر
٤ يستجوب الشاهد	٥ قال الحقيقة	٦ بقي هنا

Now make all your proposals negative:

e.g.: ذهب ← لا نذهب، لا تذهب، لا يذهبوا

lā nadhhab, lā tadhhab, lā yadhhabū

Exercise 3. Recast, without topic-and-comment structure:

e.g.: البرنامج الفضائي يستمرّون فيه بالرغم من المشاكل.

← يستمرّون في البرنامج الفضائي بالرغم من المشاكل.

yastamirrūna fi-l-barnāmaj al-faḍā'ī bi-r-raghm min al-mashākil.

١ المطر نفهم جميعنا أهمّيته من أجل القطاع الزراعي.
٢ حقيقة حكاية الشاهد نشكّ فيها شكّاً عميقاً.
٣ النيل العظيم لن ننساه أبداً.
٤ المحيط الهندي رئيته لأوّل مرّة وأنا ولد صغير.
٥ الخليج العربي هل تعرف منطقته؟
٦ جدول أعمال اليوم قد وضع الأمين نقطتين عليه.

Exercise 4. Express a wish for the action or situation:

e.g.: يوافق الطرفان على هذه النقطة. ← لو وافق الطرفان على ...

law wāfaq aṭ-ṭarafān 'ala hādhihi n-nuqṭa.

١ يكون السلام في المنطقة. ٢ لا تمطر السماء.
٣ يصير الطقس أحسن. ٤ لا يكذبون.
٥ لينتظروا أكثر. ٦ لم أنس اسم وعنوانهم.

Exercise 5. Read this report, deducing the meaning of those words marked '†'. Give the report your own title:

غطت(1) الثلوج بعض مرتفعات دولة الإمارات العربية المتّحدة في اليومين الأخيرين وانخفضت درجة الحرارة دون† الصفر(2) في بعض المناطق. كما أكّدت وسائل الإعلام(3) المحلّية مشيرةً إلى أنّها المرّة الأولى الّتي تشهد فيها البلاد الثلوج.

وقالت الصحف الّتي نشرت صوراً لمناطق إماراتية مغطاة بالثلوج "في حالة نادرة(4) الحدوث(5) اكتست(6) المرتفعات الجبلية وخصوصاً في إمارة رأس الخيمة(7) بالثلوج فيما انخفضت درجات الحرارة دون الصفر." وأضاف أنّ "كمّيات كبيرة من الثلج تجمعت(8) أثّر(9) تساقطها(10) ليل† الثلاثاء - الأربعاء على مساحات(11) واسعة من المرتفعات الجبلية، خصوصاً† في جبل جيس(12) الّذي يبعد† ٢٥ كيلومتراً شمال مدينة رأس الخيمة" شمال شرق الإمارات.

(from الحياة *Al-Hayat* newspaper, 31.12.2004)

(1) غطا يغطو *ghaṭa yaghṭū* I to cover (2) صفر *ṣifr* zero
(3) وسائل إعلام *wasā'il 'i'lām* media (4) نادر *nādir* rare
(5) حدوث *ḥudūth* occurrence
(6) اكتسى ب *iktása* VIII *bi-* to be clothed with/in
(7) رأس الخيمة *ra's al-khayma* Ras al Khayma
(8) تجمّع *tajamma'a* V to be accumulated
(9) أثّر على *'aththara* II *'ala* to affect
(10) تساقط *tasāquṭ* fall (e.g. of snow) (11) مساحة *misāḥa* area
(12) جبل جيس *jabal jays* Jebel Jays (1900 m.)

Now explain how you deduced the meaning of each word marked '†'.

14 Revision – 2

- Structures

Exercise 1. Complete the sentence, using the parenthesised words, altering them as appropriate:

e.g.: احتجّوا (احتجاج، شديد) ← احتجّوا احتجاجًا شديداً.

iḥtajjū ḥtijājan shadīdan.

١ غاب اليوم (سيادة، سفير)
٢ كان احتجاجهم (شديد، لهجة)
٣ في الماضي كان التجّار يسافرون (ركب، إبل)
٤ دخلت الشرطة البيت وهم (حمل، أسلحة، خفيف)
٥ تنازل المؤمّن عليه عن التعويض (وفق، مادّه، ثالث)
٦ لا يفيدنا كثيراً أنّه يشرح العملية (شرح، طويل، فنّي)
٧ لا يمكنك إلغاء العقد و(المفاوضات، جار)
٨ كان يجب أن يوقفوا البحوث (نظر، غيبة، وزير)
٩ قد أطلقوا أمس صاروخًا (عظيم، قوة، تمهيد، طيران، قمر)
١٠ إنّنا ننصح لكم (هذا، عمل، صفة، محاموكم)
١١ ألقى وزير المالية خطابه (نام، نصف، نوّاب، حاضر)
١٢ يجب أن ندرس الاتّهام (دراسة، كامل)

Now mark and explain all the accusative forms used.

Exercise 2. Complete the sentence with an accusative expression:

e.g.: تمّ تنفيذ الإجراء ... أوّل تمّوز.

← تمّ تنفيذ الإجراء اعتباراً من\ابتداءً من أوّل تمّوز.

tamm tanfīdh al-'ijrā' i'tibāran min/ibtidā'an min 'awwal tammūz.

١ حضّروا حفلة استقبال مقدّمةً ... القائم بالأعمال السابق.
٢ نطبّق هذا الإجراء ... البند الرابع من الاتّفاقية.
٣ قاموا بتوظيف عمّال إضافيين ... تأخير المشروع.
٤ قاموا بتوظيف عمّال إضافيين ... إنجاز المشروع.
٥ وقّع مدير المبيعات ... المدير العامّ.
٦ قد نشرت الوكالة إعلانها ... اقتراح الحكومة غير المقبول.

٧ تمّت مراجعة جميع الأرقام ... اجتماع القمّة في الشهر المقبل.
٨ فليرسلوا طلبًا ... جهود أعضاء الحركة من أجل إلغاء الخطّة.

Now take your answers and substitute your own words for everything following the accusative expression:

e.g.: تمّ تنفيذ الإجراء اعتباراً من أوّل تمّوز.
← تمّ تنفيذ الإجراء اعتباراً من تاريخ افتتاح المعهد.
tamm tanfīdh al-'ijrā' i'tibāran min tārīkh iftitāḥ al-ma'had.

Exercise 3. Make an exclamation:

e.g.: *mā 'a'ẓam as-safīna.* سفينة – عظيم ← ما أعظم السفينة.

١ هو – قوي   ٢ نموذج – بسيط
٣ هي – مفيد   ٤ هذه القضية – طويل
٥ أطفاله – كبير   ٦ نقود – خسرنا

Exercise 4. Replace the simple verb with a verb + verbal noun:

e.g.: *tamm 'iṭlāq aṣ-ṣārūkh.* أُطلق الصاروخ. ← تمّ إطلاق الصاروخ.

١ أعطت الوكالة عون الطوارئ.
٢ فُتّش المثقب عندما انفجرت البئر.
٣ نفّذوا الجزء الآخر من البرنامج قبل ابتداء الأمطار.
٤ تؤمّن هذه الشركة بصورة رئيسية حالات الكوارث الطبيعية.
٥ لم تُوقّع الاتّفاقية إلاّ بعد بحوث طويلة ومعقّدة.
٦ يقاوم الفدائيون قوات احتلال أرضهم.

Exercise 5. Add يا or أيّها\أيتها:

e.g.: الأصدقاء الأعزّاء ← أيّها الأصدقاء الأعزّاء
'ayyuha l-'aṣdiqā' al-'a'izzā'

١ أستاذي   ٢ سيادة السفير
٣ متخرّجات ومتخرّجو الكلّية   ٤ الإخوان الأعضاء
٥ إخوان أعضاء الهيئة القنصلية

Exercise 6. Make two enlargements (125%) of this data sheet. Guess or look up the new words, find the information and fill the copies in for

(a) Jordan and (b) United Arab Emirates:

البلاد: .... الدستور: ....

المساحة: ....كم² عدد السكّان: ....

اللغات: .... الأديان: ....

سنة استقلاله: .... العيد الوطني: ....

عضوية منظّمات دولية رئيسية: ....

....

الوحدة النقدية: .... قيمتها: ......\$ ، ......\€

العاصمة: .... عدد سكّان العاصمة: ....

المدن الرئيسية الأخرى: ....

الموانئ الرئيسية: ....

المنتجات المعدنية\الأولية: ....

المنتجات الصناعية: ....

المنتجات الزراعية: ....

قطاع الخدمات: ....

Exercise 7. Give the opposite in meaning, keeping the structure:

e.g.: قرض بفائدة منخفضة ← قرض بفائدة مرتفعة

qarḍ bi-fā'ida murtafi'a

١ عقود طويلة الأجل ٢ على الأقلّ

٣ تكاليف الاستثمار ٤ الدخل السنوي

٥ تدريب نظري ٦ أطفال أقوياء الجسم

Exercise 8. Recast, with improper agreement:

e.g.: شركة ذات مال كبير ← شركة كبيرة المال *sharika kabīra l-māl*

١ بلاد له عضوية دائمة ٢ الصواريخ بمجال طويل

٣ دولة اقتصادها ضعيف ٤ لأساتذة ذوي علم واسع

٥ مع المرشّح بالأهلية المناسبة ٦ تجارب بنتائج ممتازة

Exercise 9. Join the second sentence as a clause of circumstance:

e.g.: قد قرأ الوثيقة. رجعنا من المجلس.

← قد قرأ الوثيقة ونحن نرجع من المجلس.

qad qara' al-wathīqa wa-naḥnu narji' min al-majlis.

١ ارسلوا خبرا شفويا بتعليمات. لا تكفينا التعليمات ابدا.

٢ كيف نتصل بهم؟ اننا لا نعرف عنوانهم الجديد.

٣ ان اقتراحهم عظيم. لنشكرهم ولنجاوب جوابا ايجابيا.

٤ يطلب السكان الحكم الذاتي. ترفض الحكومة مثل هذا التطور.

٥ يقود وفدنا سيادة السفير. يعرف سيادته جدول الأعمال تماما.

Exercise 10. Study this text and answer the questions:

مقاليد(1) السلطة في إيران

المرشد(2) الأعلى آية الله علي خامنئي (*'āyat ullāh 'alī khāmini'ī*): يعيّن مدى(3) الحياة وسلطته فوق جميع السلطات.

مجلس صيانة(4) الدستور: يعيّن خامنئي نصف(5) أعضائه، ولديه صلاحية(6) مراجعة المرشّحين للانتخابات والقوانين قبل إقرارها.(7)

الرئيس (...) : منتخب لمدّة ٤ سنوات لكن بوسع (8) رجال الدين تعطيل(9) سلطته.

البرلمان: مؤلّف(10) من ٢٩٠ نائبًا ومن صلاحيته اقتراح القوانين وتمريرها،(11) شريطةً(12) موافقة جهات أخرى.

(from a BBC broadcast, 2.2.04)

(1) مقاليد *maqālīd* (inan. pl.) reins

(2) مرشد *murshid* guide

(3) (الـ)مدى *madan (al-mada)* (wk.) extent

(4) صيانة *ṣiyāna* preservation (here: guardianship)

(5) نصف أنصاف *niṣf 'anṣāf* half

(6) صلاحية *ṣalāḥīya* competence

(7) إقرار *'iqrār* confirmation

(8) وسع *wus'* capability

(9) تعطيل *ta'ṭīl* suspension

(10) مؤلّف *mu'allaf* composed

(11) تمرير *tamrīr* passing

(12) شريطةً *sharīṭatan* subject to

١ لمن أعلى سلطة في إيران؟ هو مؤيّن لأيّة مدّة؟

٢ اشرح دور مجلس صيانة الدستور ودور البرلمان.

15 Correspondence

- Formal and informal letters

1. Formal letters

Read this example of a formal letter:

شركة "الوطن" المحدودة للتأمين

بيروت في ٤ تمّوز ٢٠٠٥

السيّد حسّن عبده
قسم التعويضات

تحية طيّبة وبعد
يسرّني بأنّي أخبركم بإجراء قرّره مجلس الإدارة أخيراً وستقوم بترقيتكم من رتبة مفتّش إلى مفتّش رئيسي درجة أولى ابتداءً من أوّل آب سنة ٢٠٠٥.
وتنتج الترقية المذكورة عن خبرتكم وجهودكم في خدمة الشركة ويهنّئكم مجلس الإدارة على هذه الترقية المستحقّة.

وتفضّلوا بقبول فائق الاحترام

المخلص

زين عبد الرحمن
مدير قسم شؤون الموظّفين

نسخة إلى: قسم المحاسبات

as-sayyid ḥassan ʿabdu Mr Hassan Abdo

qism at-taʿwīḍāt	Claims ('Compensation') Dept.
taḥīya ṭayyiba wa-baʿdu	Dear Sir
yusurrunī bi-'annī 'ukhbirukum	I am pleased to inform you of
bi-'ijrā' qarrarahu majlis	the measure agreed recently
al-'idāra 'akhīran wa-sa-taqūm	by the Board of Directors to
bi-tarqīyatikum min rutbat mufattish	promote you from Inspector to
'ila mufattish ra'īsī daraja 'ūla	Chief Inspector Grade One with
btidā'an min 'awwal 'āb sanat 2005.	effect from 1st August 2005.
wa-tantij at-tárqiya l-madhkūra ʿan	This promotion results from your
khibratikum wa-juhūdikum fī khidmat	experience and your diligence in
ash-sharika wa yuhanni'ukum majlis	the company's service and the
al-'idāra ʿala hādhihi t-tárqīya	Board of Directors congratulates
l-mustaḥaqqa.	you on this deserved promotion.
wa-tafaḍḍalū bi-qabūl fā'iq	Please accept the highest
al-iḥtirām	respect
al-mukhliṣ	Sincerely ('the sincere')
zayn ʿabd ar-raḥmān	Zein Abdulrahman
mudīr qism shu'ūn al-muwaẓẓafīn	Personnel Manager
nuskha 'ila: qism al-muḥasabāt	Copy to: Accounting Department

Note:

- The standard opening formula is

  تحية طيّبة وبعد *taḥīya ṭayyiba wa-baʿdu*

  تحية is 'greeting', but the phrase as used here allows no exact translation; its equivalent is 'Dear Sir/Madam'. The text of the letter follows immediately.
- The أنتم form of verbs, possessives and pronouns is often used for politeness, as are the deferential forms (Chapter 11).
- فايق الاحترام 'exceeding respect' in the formal closure may be replaced by other expressions as appropriate, e.g.:

  وتفضّلوا بقبول وافر الشكر *(wāfir ash-shukr)*

  Please accept abundant thanks
- المخلص\المخلصة *al-mukhliṣ(a)* may be added to the formal

closure. In some letters it may replace it, and may take the form وأظلّ مخلصًا\مخلصةً *wa-'aẓall mukhliṣan/mukhliṣatan* ('and I remain sincere') Sincerely

2. Informal letters

Read this example of an informal letter:

دمشق في ٢٠ تشرين الثاني ٢٠٠٥

اخي كامل العزيز
تحية طيبة وبعد
كما اتفقنا اكتب لك شيئاً حول الوظيفة الجديدة. كل شيء ماشي جيدا
ولكني اعترف بمشاكل كانت توجد في الابتداء. كنت اجلس امام
كمبيوتر لم ار مثله ابدا وطلبوا ان اعالج كمية ضخمة من المعطيات
التجارية وهذا باستعمال برنامج معقد الإجراءات.
على كل حال ساعدني زميل جديد وفي النهاية نجحنا الحمد لله.
كيف شغلك انت؟ ان شاء الله طيب.
سأتصل بك بعد ايام قليلة.
تحياتي لمريم وللجميع
المخلص

'akhi kāmil al-'azīz	Dear ('My dear brother') Kamil
taḥīya ṭayyiba wa-ba'du	
kama ttafaqna 'aktub laka shay'an ḥawl al-waẓīfa l-jadīda. kull shay' māshī jayyidan walākinnī 'a'tárif bi-mashākil kānat tūjad fi l-ibtidā'.	As agreed I am writing you something about the new job. Everything is going well but I admit that there were problems ('to problems that there were') in the beginning.
kunt 'ajlis 'amām kambyūtir lam 'ara mithlahu 'abadan wa-ṭalabū 'an 'u'ālij kammīya ḍakhma min	I sat in front of a computer the like of which I had never seen and they asked me to process a

al-muʿṭayāt at-tijārīya wa-hādha bi-stiʿmāl barnāmaj muʿaqqad al-'ijrā'āt. ʿala kull ḥāl sā'adanī zamīl jadīd wa-bi-n-nihāya najaḥna l-ḥamdu li-llah.

vast amount of commercial data, all ('and that') using a programme with complicated procedures. Anyway ('In any case') a new colleague helped me and finally we succeeded, thank heaven ('praise (be) to God').

kayf shughluka 'anta? 'inshallah ṭayyib.

How is your work? All right, I hope (B37).

sa-'attásil bika baʿd 'ayyām qalīla. taḥīyātī li-maryam wa-li-l-jamīʿ. al-mukhliṣ, 'aḥmad.

I will get in touch with you in a few days. My regards to Mariam and to all. Sincerely, Ahmad

Note:

- The letter usually opens with a personal greeting such as:

  أخي (كامل) العزيز\الكريم (*al-karīm* kind) Dear Kamil

  أختي مريم العزيزة\الكريمة *'ukhtī maryam al-ʿazīza/al-karīma* Dear Maryam

  أستاذي المحترم (*l-muḥtáram*) Dear ('Respected') Professor

  زملائي الكرماء (*l-kuramā'*) Dear ('Kind') Colleagues

  followed by the obligatory opening formula تحية طيّبة وبعد.
- المخلص\المخلصة is optional, and may be preceded by a personal closure like the one shown above or, e.g.:

  ويسلّم\تسلّم عليك\عليكم *wa-yusallim/tusallim ʿalayka/ʿalayki/ʿalaykum* Regards from (سلّم على II to greet)

3. Vocabulary: المراسلة والكمبيوترات

al-murāsala wa-l-kambyūtirāt

Correspondence and computers

إجراء *'ijrā'* (also:) procedure

اختار *ikhtāra* VIII to select

أخلص	*'akhlaṣa* IV to be sincere, loyal
أرفق (ب)	*'arfaqa* IV *(bi-)* to enclose (with)
أسطوانة أساطين	*'usṭuwāna 'asāṭīn* disk
إشارة	*'ishāra* reference (number)
بالإشارة إلى	*bi-l-'ishāra 'ila* with reference to
أطفأ	*'aṭfa'a* IV to switch off
آلة مسح	*'ālat masḥ* scanner
برامج	*barāmij* (inan. pl., also:) software
برمجة	*barmaja* programming
بياني	*bayānī* graphical
تهنئة تهانئ	*tahni'a tahāni'* congratulation
جهاز أجهزة	*jihāz 'ajhiza* appliance, apparatus
جهاز تدوير	*jihāz tadwīr* drive (disk etc.)
جهاز مسح	*jihāz masḥ* scanner
حاسب	*ḥāsib* calculator
حذف يحذف	*ḥadhafa yaḥdhifu* I to delete
حرّر	*ḥarrara* II (also:) to edit
خزن يخزن\خزّن	*khazana yakhzunu* I, *khazzana* II to store
خطاب أخطبة	*khiṭāb 'akhṭiba* (also:) letter
ذاكرة	*dhākira* memory
ربط يربط (ب)	*rabaṭa yarbuṭu (bi-)* I to connect (with/to)
رداً على	*raddan 'ala* in reply to
رسم رسوم	*rasm rusūm* drawing, graph
سكّر	*sakkara* II to shut
صندوق بريدي (ص.ب)	*ṣandūq barīdī* post office box (POB)
صوّر	*ṣawwara* II (also:) to photocopy
ضخم ضخام	*ḍakhm ḍikhām* vast
طابع	*ṭābi'* printer
طبع	*ṭab'* printing
عاجل	*'ājil* urgent

عرض يعرض *'araḍa ya'riḍu* I to display, to show
عرض عروض *'arḍ 'urūḍ* display
غلط أغلاط *ghalaṭ 'aghlāṭ* error
فاق يفوق *fāqa yafūqu* I to exceed
فتح يفتح *fataḥa yaftaḥu* I (also:) to switch on
كريم كرماء *karīm kuramā'* kind, generous
لوحة ألواح *lawḥa 'alwāḥ* board
لوّن *lawwana* II to colour
لون ألوان *lawn 'alwān* colour
مسح يمسح *masaḥa yamsaḥu* I to scan
معالجة النصوص *mu'ālajat an-nuṣūṣ* wordprocessing
نسخ ينسخ *nasakha yansakhu* I to copy
هنّأ (على) *hanna'a* II *('ala)* to congratulate (on)
وصل يصل (ب) *waṣala yaṣilu* I *(bi-)* (also:) to connect (to)
وفر يفر *wafara yafiru* I to abound

Exercise 1. Read this announcement posted on a factory noticeboard:

من: قسم الأمن
التاريخ: ٢٥\٥\٦.

إلى: جميع الأقسام؛ الألواح
الإشارة: أمن ٣٦٥

الموضوع: أشغال على المدخل الشمالي

يشير قسم الأمن إلى مذكّرته رقم ٣٦٢ من ١٤\٥\٦. ويؤكّد أن المدخل الشمالي (جنب قسم الهندسة) سيظلّ مسكّراً خلال شهر حزيران الكامل وذلك من أجل إنجاز أشغال بنائية ضرورية. وخلال المدّة المذكورة سيظلّ مفتوحاً المدخل الرئيسي فقط. إن إعادة استعمال المدخل الشمالي مخطّطة في أوائل شهر تمّوز وسيعلن بواسطة إعلان خاصّ في وقت مناسب.

مدير قسم الأمن

Write the announcement referred to in the last sentence, with appropriate date and references.

Exercise 2. Write a letter to Claims Department at Al-Watan Insurance Company saying that you have not received an answer to your claim for reimbursement sent to them a month ago.

Exercise 3. Arrange these computer operations in chronological order:

١ أطفئ الطابع.
٢ اكتب نصّاً جديداً أو حرّر نصّاً سابقًا.
٣ أطفئ الكمبيوتر
٤ اختر تفاصيل الطبع – كم نسخةً؟ ملوّن أم أسود وأبيض؟
٥ صل الكمبيوتر بالكهربا.
٦ اخزن نصّك الجديد أو المحرّر.
٧ افتح الكمبيوتر.
٨ صل الطابع ووضع الورق فيه.
٩ افتح برنامج معالجة النصوص.
١٠ اطبع نصّك.

Exercise 4. Here are typical ASDFG... lines of keys, one from a computer and one from a typewriter. Which is which, and why?

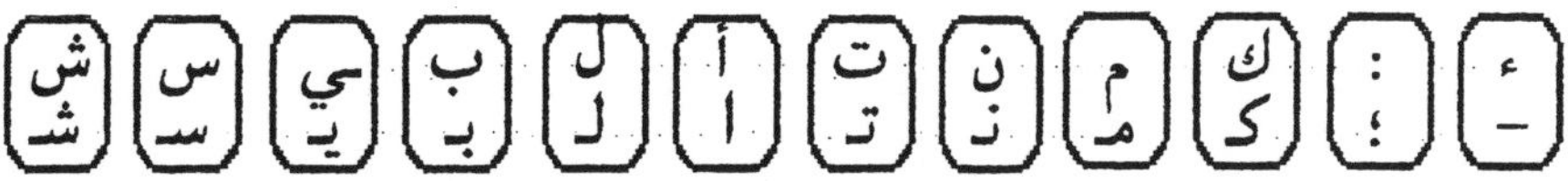

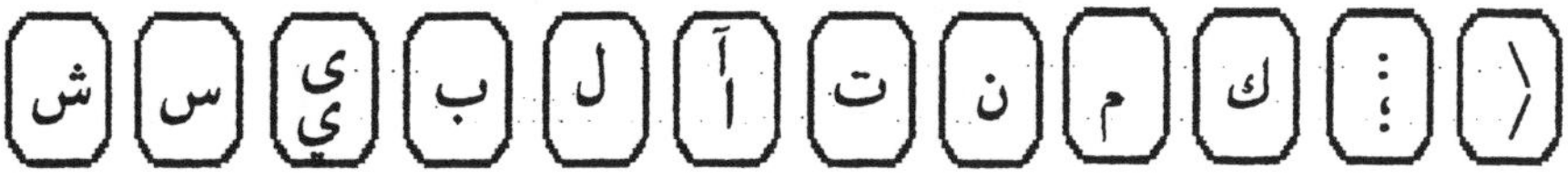

Exercise 5. You are on holiday in Cairo. Write a short letter to an Arab friend who does not know Egypt, describing an interesting visit or excursion. Mention other things which you plan to see. (Get help from tourist literature if necessary.)

Exercise 6. Respond positively to this letter:

ص.ب. ٢٤٨٢
دبي في ٦/٦/٣٠.

اصدقائي الكرماء
تحية طيبة وبعد

وصلت الى الإمارات وكل شيء درجة اولى. بدأت مهمتي في المعهد وجميع الزملاء والمدير ناس لطفاء جدا. ظروف العمل ممتازة ويسرني كثيرا بأن اخترت مهمة في دبي. عندي مشكلة صغيرة ارجوكم مساعدتكم لحلها. عند المغادرة تركت كتاب التعليمات لآلتي للتصوير الرقمي† ولا اجد نسخة هنا. هل يمكنكم إرسال هذا الكتاب بالبريد الجوي؟ اكون ممنونا جدا. تجدونه في محلي في المختبر.
عنواني البريدي مكتوب فوق.
ان شاء الله كل شيء طيب عندكم. كيف كانت حفلة الأستاذ؟ سلم عليه من طرفي. سأكتب له خطابا خاصا بعد قليل.
تحياتي وشكري للجميع
المخلص

محمد

† *'ālatī li-t-taṣwīr ar-raqmī* - deduce its meaning; you know the roots.

16 Numbers - 1

- Literary form of the cardinal numbers

1. General

In B 38 we studied the simplified pronunciation of the cardinal numbers. You should continue to use this pronunciation.

In this chapter we examine the literary or official spelling and grammar of the cardinal numbers written as words, with their (now less common) formal pronunciation which we show in braces { } where it differs substantially from the simplified form. The columns show the numbers used with a quantified noun. In counting with no stated or implied noun, the masculine form (i.e. the left-hand column) is used.

In the following, the rules given in B 38 apply, unless stated otherwise.

2. Numbers 1 to 10

	quantifying a m. noun		quantifying a f. noun	
١	واحد	*wāḥid*	واحدة	*wāḥida*
٢	اثنان\ين	*{ithnān} -ayn*	اثنتان\ين	*{ithnatān, -ayn}*
٣	ثلاثة	*thalātha*	ثلاث	*{thalāth}*
٤	أربعة	*'arba'a*	أربع	*{'arba'}*
٥	خمسة	*khamsa*	خمس	*{khams}*
٦	ستة	*sitta*	ست	*{sitt}*
٧	سبعة	*sab'a*	سبع	*{sab'}*
٨	ثمانية	*thamāniya*	ثمان\ثماني	*{thamānin, thamānī}*
٩	تسعة	*tis'a*	تسع	*{tis'}*
١٠	عشرة	*'ashara*	عشر	*{'ashr}*

Note:

- The literary forms of 2 have the endings of dual adjectives.
- Numbers 1, 3 to 7, 9 and 10 have regular case-endings in full pronunciation.
- Number 8 has regular case-endings in full pronunciation for the

form ثمانية. But the form ثمان is weak; it becomes ثماني (*thamānī* nom. and gen., *thamāniya* acc.) before a noun.

- Numbers 3 to 10 have so-called *polarity* or *polarised agreement*, i.e. the number has an apparently fem. form when used with a masc. quantified noun, and an apparently masc. form for quantifying a fem. noun. The polarity applies both in indefinite and definite expressions:

على اللوحة ثلاث دوائر. *'ala l-lawḥa {**thalāth**} dawā'ir.*
(f . noun) There are three circuits on the board.

الدوائر الثلاث للوحة *ad-dawā'ir ath-{**thalāth**} li-l-lawḥa* the three circuits on ('of') the board

للمحرّك أربعة تروس أمامية. *li-l-muḥarrik '**arba'a** turūs 'amāmīya.* (m. noun + adj.) The engine has four forward gears.

التروس الأربعة الأمامية للمحرّك *at-turūs al-'**arba'a** l-'amāmīya li-l-muḥarrik* the engine's four forward gears

With 3 to 10, in the indefinite expression the noun (+ adjective if any) is always *genitive plural* (regardless of its function in the sentence); but in the definite expression the noun or noun expression is in the case dictated by its function in the sentence.

3. Numbers 11 to 99

	quantifying a m. noun		quantifying a f. noun	
١١	أحد عشر	*{'aḥad 'ashar}*	إحدى عشرة	*{'iḥda 'ashra}*
١٢	اثنا عشر\اثني عشر	*{ithna 'ashar, ithnay 'ashar}*	اثنتا عشرة\اثنتي عشرة	*{ithnata 'ashra, ithnatay 'ashra}*
١٣	ثلاثة عشر	*{thalāthat 'ashar}*	ثلاث عشرة	*{thalāth 'ashra}*
١٤	أربعة عشر	*'arba'at 'ashar*	أربع عشرة	*{'arba' 'ashra}*
١٥	خمسة عشر	*khamsat 'ashar*	خمس عشرة	*{khams 'ashra}*
١٦	ستّة عشر	*{sittat 'ashar}*	ستّ عشرة	*{sitt 'ashra}*
١٧	سبعة عشر	*sab'at 'ashar*	سبع عشرة	*{sab' 'ashra}*
١٨	ثمانية عشر	*{thamāniyat 'ashar}*	ثماني عشرة	*{thamānī 'ashra}*
١٩	تسعة عشر	*tis'at 'ashar*	تسع عشرة	*{tis' 'ashra}*

quantifying any noun

٢٠	عشرون\ين	{'ishrūn} -īn	٣٠	ثلاثون\ين	{thalāthūn} -īn
٤٠	أربعون\ين	{'arba'ūn} -īn	٥٠	خمسون\ين	{khamsūn} -īn
٦٠	ستون\ين	{sittūn} -īn	٧٠	سبعون\ين	{sab'ūn} -īn
٨٠	ثمانون\ين	{thamānūn} -īn	٩٠	تسعون\ين	{tis'ūn} -īn

Note:

- In numbers 11 and 12 both elements have regular gender agreement with the quantified noun; in numbers 13 to 19 the units have polarised agreement, while the tens have regular agreement.
- Of the 'teens, only the number 12 changes for case (ا... *-a* nom., ي... *-ay* acc./gen.).
- The tens follow the masculine sound plural pattern for case. They do not change for gender.
- The last sentence of paragraph 2 above applies for numbers 11 to 99 if we substitute *accusative singular* for '*genitive plural*' and *case and number* for 'case':

  دلّ المقياس على خمسين فولتًا. *dall al-miqyās 'ala khamsīn voltan.* The meter showed 50 volts. (indefinite)

  لا تكفي هذه المسامير الاثنا عشر. *la takfī hādhihi l-masāmīr al-ithna 'ashar.* These 12 rivets will not suffice. (definite)
- Compounds from 21 to 99 are assembled as described in B 38, but و is pronounced *wa-* instead of *u-*.

4. Hundreds, thousands, millions

quantifying any noun

١٠٠	مئة\مائة	{mi'a(t)}	٢٠٠	مئتان\ين	{mi'atān, -ayn}
٣٠٠	ثلاث مئة	thalāth {mi'a}	٤٠٠	أربع مئة	'arba' {mi'a}
٥٠٠	خمس مئة	khams {mi'a}	٦٠٠	ست مئة	sitt {mi'a}
٧٠٠	سبع مئة	{sab' mi'a}	٨٠٠	ثمان مئة	thamān {mi'a}
٩٠٠	تسع مئة	{tis' mi'a}	١٠٠٠	ألف	'alf
٢٠٠٠	ألفان\ين	{'alfān} -ayn	٣٠٠٠	ثلاثة آلاف	thalāthat 'ālāf
٤٠٠٠	أربعة آلاف	'arba'at 'ālāf	٥٠٠٠	خمسة آلاف	khamsat 'ālāf

1 million مليون *milyūn* 2 million مليونان\ين *{milyūnān} -ayn*
3, 4 million ثلاثة\أربعة ملايين *thalātha, 'arba'a malāyīn*
100 million مئة مليون *{mi'at} milyūn*

Note:

- مئة is a feminine noun and the number preceding it has therefore no ending ة... . After 3 to 9, مئة always stands in the *genitive singular*, and the compound may be written as one word or two.
- ألف and مليون are masculine nouns and the number preceding them therefore has the ending ة... . After 3 to 9, ألف or مليون always stands in the *genitive plural.*
- The indeterminate plurals of مئة, ألف and مليون are مئات *mi'āt*, ألوف *'ulūf* and ملايين *malāyīn.*
- In indefinite expressions, the noun quantified by مئة, ألف or مليون stands in the *genitive singular*, forming an indefinite singular construct with it. In definite expressions, the noun stands in the case and number demanded by its function in the sentence:

خمس مئة دينار *khams {mi'at} dīnār* 500 dinars
نفس الدنانير الخمسمئة *nafs ad-danānīr {al-khamsmi'a}* the same 500 dinars

5. Vocabulary: الهندسة *al-handasa* Engineering

NB: see also the text of Chapter 2 for other technical vocabulary

إلى الأمام *'ila l-'amām* forwards
أنبوب أنابيب *'unbūb 'anābīb* pipe, tube
برغي براغي *burghī barāghī* screw
بطّارية *baṭṭārīya* battery
بلاستيك *blāstīk* plastic
ترس تروس *tirs turūs* gear(wheel)
حديد *ḥadīd* iron
دايرة دوائر *dā'ira dawā'ir* (also:) circuit
دولاب دواليب *dūlāb dawālīb* wheel

ديزل	*dīzil* diesel
زجاج	*zujāj* glass
شحّم	*shaḥḥama* II to lubricate
شحن	*shaḥn* load
شحن يشحن	*shaḥana yashḥanu* I to load; to charge (battery)
صامولة صواميل	*ṣāmūla ṣawāmīl* nut
صلّح	*ṣallaḥa* II to repair
صمام	*ṣimām* valve, plug
صهريج صهاريج	*ṣahrīj ṣahārīj* tank (fuel etc.)
ضخّ يضخّ	*ḍakhkha yaḍukhkhu* I to pump
علامة	*'alāma* signal, mark, sign
فولاذ	*fūlādh* steel
فولت\ڤولت	*volt* volt
قاس يقيس	*qāsa yaqīsu* I to measure
مولّد	*muwallid* generator
واط	*wāṭ* watt
إلى الوراء	*'ila l-warā'* backwards
وقود	*wuqūd* fuel

Exercise 1. Write the expression in words; read your answer in literary style, marking this where it differs from the simplified form:

e.g.: ٢٥٠٠ (برميل) ← ألفا وخمس مئة\خمسمئة برميل

{'alfā wa-khams mi'at} barmīl

١ ٣٥ (طنّ)

٢ ١٥ (واط)

٣ بـ ٤ (دولاب)

٤ (البرميل) الـ ٥٠٠

٥ مركّب بواسطة ٦ (برغي)

٦ شحن ٢٠٠٠ (طنّ)

٧ أقلّ من (طنّ) الـ ٥ المطلوبة

٨ سلك حامل ١٢ (ڤولت)

٩ ٨ (لتر) بنزين و٢٠ من الديزل

١٠ يكلّف ٣٣ (ريال).

Exercise 2. Make indefinite expressions definite, and vice versa, writing the numbers in words:

e.g.: خمسة وعشرون لتراً ← اللترات الخمسة وعشرون
al-litrāt al-khamsa wa-{'ishrūn}

١ دفع الدنانير المئتين
٢ المحركات الستّة الجديدة
٣ ثلاث طلمبات قوية
٤ في كلّ الدواليب الأربعة
٥ ٢٤ صامولة بلاستيكية
٦ اثنا عشرة أشهر
٧ خلال أربع وعشرين ساعةً
٨ في صهريج ذي ٣٠٠ لتر

Exercise 3. Read how to check the engine oil. Deduce and explain the words marked '†', and summarise the passage in your own words:

محرّك الديزل: مراجعة مستوى زيت المحرّك

١ أوقف السيارة على سطح(1) أفقي(2) بعد وصول المحرّك لدرجة حرارة التشغيل، أي بعد السير† بالسيارة دون توقّف† المسافة(3) لا تقلّ† عن ١٠ كم.

٢ أوقف المحرّك.

٣ أخرج† عصا(4) قياس† الزيت بعد حوالي ٥ دقائق وامسحها† بخرقة(5) لا ينسل(6) نسيجها(7) أو بمنديل(8) ورقي أو ما شابه† ذلك.

٤ أدخل† عصا القياس بعناية(9) داخل أنبوب القياس حتّى النهاية، ثمّ أخرجها مرّة أخرى. يجب أن يكون مستوى الزيت بين العلامتين على عصا القياس.

تبلغ كمّية الزيت بين العلامتين على العصا القياس حوالي لتراً واحداً*.

ولا يجوز أن يرتفع الزيت فوق مستوى العلامة العليا الموجودة على عصا القياس. فالزيت الزائد عن الحدّ يضرّ المحرّك.

(from the BMW Series 3 User's Manual, by permission of BMW)

(1) سطح سطوح *saṭḥ suṭūḥ* surface (2) أفقي *'ufuqī* horizontal
(3) مسافة *masāfa* distance (4) عصا عصي *'aṣa 'uṣī* (f.) stick
(5) خرقة خرق *khirqa khiraq* rag (6) نسل ينسل *nasala yansulu* I to fray
(7) نسيج أنسجة *nasīj 'ansija* texture
(8) منديل مناديل *mandīl manādīl* handkerchief (9) عناية *'ināya* care

* Comment on the phrase حوالي لتراً واحداً .

17 Numbers – 2

- Text numbering
- Fractions
- Calculations and measurements

1. Text numbering

In European script it is common to use alphabetical letters or Roman numerals to number sections of text.

Arabic uses alphabetical letters for this purpose. Every letter has a numerical value, but we need to know only the first ten. The common mnemonic device for these is أبجد هوّز حطي *'abjad hawwaz ḥuṭī*. أبجد means 'alphabet'; the other words have no meaning:

10 9 8   7 6 5   4 3 2 1

أ بـجـد هـو ز حـطـي

In this use ا is almost always written with its *hamza*, avoiding confusion with the number ١.

It is also common to use the adverbial forms of ordinal numbers (B 38):

أولاً *awwalan* ('firstly') 1, I, i, A, a

ثانياً *thānīyan* ('secondly') 2, II, ii, B, b (etc.)

Typical text numbering:

أولاً – القرينة العامّة	
'awwalan – al-qarīna l-ʿāmma	I – General Context
١ المقدّمة والمبادئ الأساسية	1 Introduction and basic principles
٢ الأنظار الرئيسية:	2 *(al-'anẓār)* Main considerations:
أ الفنّية	(a)/(i) Technical
ب المالية	(b)/(ii) Financial
ج الاجتماعية	(c)/(iii) Social
د القانونية	(d)/(iv) Legal
هـ المتعلّقة بالبيئة	(e)/(v) *(bi-l-bī'a)* Environmental
٣ وضع الشركة	3 Company position

2. Fractions

Denominators 2 to 10, all masculine nouns, are as follows. All except 'half' are derived from the corresponding cardinal number:

نصف أنصاف *niṣf 'anṣāf* half   ثلث أثلاث *thulth 'athlāth* third
ربع أرباع *rub' 'arbā'* quarter   خمس أخماس *khums 'akhmās* fifth
سدس أسداس *suds 'asdās* sixth   سبع أسباع *sub' 'asbā'* seventh
ثمن أثمان *thumn 'athmān* eighth   تسع أتساع *tus' 'atsā'* ninth
عشر أعشار *'ushr 'a'shār* tenth

في نصفي الحساب *fī niṣfay al-ḥisāb*
in both halves of the calculation
ثلثا طلاّبنا *(thulthā)* two thirds of our students
حتّى خمسة أثمان منها *(khamsat 'athmān)* up to $\frac{5}{8}$ of them
ستة وربع *(wa-rub')* six and a quarter

Remember (B 38) that even in simplified pronunciation a final ة... on a number is pronounced *-at* before a noun beginning with ...أ.

Fractions with a denominator higher than 10 are constructed with على or من *min* and the cardinal number:

خمسة على\من اثني عشر *khamsa 'ala/min ithn'ashar*
('5 over 12') five twelfths

3. Calculations and measurements

Vocabulary for calculations and measurements:

حساب calculation
زيادة\إضافة\جمع *(jam')* addition
زاد يزيد (على) I to add (to)
أضاف (إلى) IV to add (to)
+ زائد + plus
مجموع *majmū'* total
طرح *ṭarḥ* subtraction
طرح يطرح (من) *ṭaraḥa yaṭraḥu* I to subtract (from)
− ناقص – minus
باق\الباقي (weak) remainder

ضرب *ḍarb* multiplication
ضرب يضرب (في) I to multiply (by)
في × × times, multiplied by
حاصل حواصل *ḥāṣil ḥawāṣil* product
قسمة *qisma* division
قسم يقسم (على) *qasama yaqsimu* I *('ala)* to divide (by)
على : ÷ divided by
كسر كسور *kasr kusūr* fraction
مربع ٢ 2 *murabba'* square(d)
مكعب ٣ 3 *muka''ab* cube(d), cubic
حجم حجوم *ḥajm ḥujūm* volume
ساوى = = *sāwa* III to equal
بالساعة\بالثانية... per hour, per second (etc.)
°م (درجة) مئوية °C *(daraja) mi'awīya* (deg.) celsius

Examples:
٢ + ٢ = ٤ *ithnayn zā'id ithnayn yusāwī 'arba'a*
٦ − ١ = ٥ *sitta nāqiṣ wāḥid yusāwī khamsa*
٨ × ٧ = ٥٦ *thamániya fī sab'a yusāwī sitta u-khamsīn*
٨١ : ٩ = ٩ *wāḥid u-thamānīn 'ala tis'a yusāwī tis'a*
مساحة ٢٧ م٢ *(mitran murabba'an)* an area of $27m^2$
حجمه ٣٦ م٣. *(mitran muka''aban)* Its volume is $36m^3$.
٧٠ كم\ساعة *sab'īn kilomitran bi-s-sā'a* 70 km/hr
٢٠٠ °م *mitay daraja mi'awīya* 200° C

In algebra – (علم) الجبر *('ilm) al-jabr*, which the Arabs taught us – أ corresponds to our 'a'. The other symbols are usually left undotted:
٢أ − ٤ب *ithnayn fī 'alif nāqiṣ 'arba'a fī bā'* 2a – 4b

4. Vocabulary: الوثائق *al-wathā'iq* Documentation

إحصاء\إحصائية *'iḥṣā', 'iḥṣā'īya* statistic(s)
أختلف (من) *ikhtálafa* VIII *(min)* to differ (from)
استنتج *istantaja* X to conclude (draw a conclusion)

تال\التالي *tālin, at-tālī* (weak) (the) following
تمهيدي *tamhīdī* provisional, preparatory
جدول جداول *jadwal jadāwil* (also:) table, chart
دفتر دفاتر *daftar dafātir* register, ledger, notebook
دليل أدلّة *dalīl 'adilla* directory
سبق يسبق *sabaqa yasbiqu* I to precede
صرّح ب *ṣarraḥa* II *bi-* to assert
عمود عواميد *'amūd 'awāmīd* column
فصل فصول *faṣl fuṣūl* chapter
فهرس فهارس *fihris fahāris* index, catalogue, list
قائمة قوائم *qā'ima qawā'im* list, register
قرينة قرائن *qarīna qarā'in* context
كاذب *kādhib* false, untrue
لاحظ *lāḥaẓa* III to comment, to annotate
مبيّضة *mubayyaḍa* fair copy
محتويات *muḥtawayāt* contents
مستند *mustanad* document, record
مسوّدة *musawwada* draft
نتج ينتج *nataja yantiju* I to result, to follow
نسبة *nisba* relation(ship), proportion
ما يلي *mā yalī* what follows
ينتج أنّ ... *yantij 'anna ...* it follows that ...

Exercise 1. Read aloud, with the numbers in simplified pronunciation:

e.g.: *thamāniya wa-thulth* ← ٨ ١/٣

١ ٪٢٥ ٢ ٣/٥ ٣ ٤ ١١/١٢

٤ ٨ م\ثانية ٥ ٩/٢٠ ٦ ٦ ٥/٧

٧ ٥ كغ\م٢ ٨ ٣٣،٣ ٩ في ٢/٣ الأمثال

١٠ حرارة ٢٠٠°م. ١١ ٩ : ٣ = ٣ ١٢ ١٠٠ - ٧٢ = ٢٨

Exercise 2. Write the expression in mathematical notation as far as possible. Point out where your pronunciation differs from the spelling:

e.g.: اثنان زائد ثمانية يساوي عشرة. ← ٢ + ٨ = ١٠

ithnayn {ithnān} zā'id thamāniya yusāwī 'ashara

١ مئة كيلومتر بالساعة
٢ ثلاثة وستّون على تسعة يساوي سبعة.
٣ بين أربعة وثلاثين وستّة وثلاثين درجة مئوية
٤ اثنان وخمسون على مئتين يساوي ستّة وعشرين بالمئة.
٥ سبعة وعشرون في ثلاثة
٦ سبعة وعشرون على ثلاثة

Exercise 3. Complete the calculations and solve the equations:

e.g.: ٢ × ٢٨ ← ٢ × ٢٨ = ٥٦

ithnayn fī thamāniya u-'ishrīn yusāwī sitta u-khamsīn.

'alif yusāwī khamsa. ١٦أ = ٨٠ ← أ = ٥

١ ١٤٪ من ٣٠٠
٢ ب٢ + ٤ = ١٣
٣ ٨م × ٤م = (مساحة)
٤ ٢٤ح - ٨ح = ٦٤
٥ ١م\ثانية = د كم\ساعة
٦ ١٨ + ٢أ = ٩٠
٧ ١١٥ - (٢ × ٦٠)
٨ ١/٢ × ٣/٤

Exercise 4. Give the opposite in meaning:

e.g.: نفى ← أكّد، صرّح ب *'akkada, ṣarraḥa bi-*

١ نتيجة ٢ مبيّضة ٣ ممّا يسبق ٤ كذّب
٥ حقيقة ٦ المدّعي ٧ الحقّ معي ٨ استلم
٩ مريض ١٠ وساخة ١١ بارد ١٢ قسمة

Exercise 5. Look at Chapter 8, Exercise 4. Do the following chain substitution in the same way, fast:

e.g.: أين توجد نمرة التلفون ؟ (مكتوب)
← أين مكتوبة نمرة التلفون؟ (عنوان الزبون)
← أين مكتوب عنوان الزبون؟ (etc.)

أ – أرسل لنا من فضلك المستند الإحصائي.

١ (لو سمحت) ٢ (الشامل) ٣ (الوثيقة)

٤ (انظر) ٥ (المحتويات) ٦ (التمهيدي)

ب – تستنتج المسوّدة استنتاجًا مقبولاً.

٧ (إيجابي) ٨ (نصّه) ٩ (يقترح) ١٠ (المعطيات)

١١ (معقّد) ١٢ (يثبت) ١٣ (الجداول) ٤١ (واضح)

Exercise 6. Examine the table, and follow the instruction:

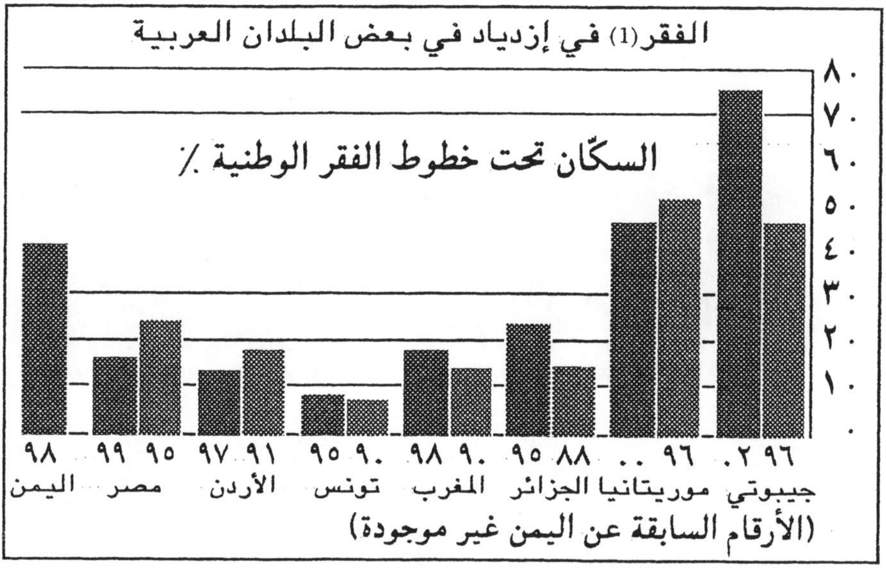

(from UNDP: Millennium Devel. Goals in Arab Countries, 2003)

(1) فقر *faqr* poverty

اشرح شفويًا(2) تفاصيل الجدول، ذاكراً على الأقلّ النقط التالية:

١ التواريخ المشار إليها ٢ التقدّم وعدم التقدّم

٣ نسبات التغيير عند بلدان مختلفة ٤ نسبة التحسّن الأفضل

٥ مقارنة بين أحسن وضع وأشدّ وضع ٦ قضية الجزائر

٧ خطّ الفقر المطبّق رسمياً عند الأمم المتّحدة (إذا عرفته)

(2) شفويًا *shafawīyan* orally

18 Revision – 3

- General

Exercise 1. Give your own definition of the word or expression:

e.g.: *maḥall li-taḥḍīr al-'akl* مطبخ ← محلّ لتحضير الأكل

١ قاض	٢ ترجمة	٣ مسوّدة
٤ قائم بالأعمال	٥ سالِم	٦ دستور
٧ قانون	٨ صور	٩ كسر
١٠ اتّفق	١١ عقد	١٢ أصلح
١٣ تكرير	١٤ معالجة النصوص	١٥ تأمين
١٦ واد	١٧ ناطق بلسان	١٨ جملة فعلية
١٩ نيابةً عن	٢٠ الشرق الأقصى	٢١ رفض
٢٢ قرن	٢٣ قرينة	٢٤ ردّ فعل

Exercise 2. Give your own answer to the condition or concession:

e.g.: *la-shtarayt sayyāratan.* لو كنت غنيًا ... ← ... لاشتريت سيّارةً.

١ إذا هو ليس حاضراً ...	٢ لو كانت عندك الأموال ...
٣ ... على شرط أن يقول الحقّ.	٤ إذا لم يعرفوا ...
٥ إذا رفضتها اللجنة ...	٦ ... لو سمحت.
٧ إذا لم يحضر زعيمهم نفسه ...	٨ حتّى ولو غاب السفير ...
٩ إذا احتجّ شخص ما ...	١٠ إذا ساوى أ ٨، ...

Exercise 3. Give the word or expression with opposite meaning:

e.g.: *jam', ziyāda, 'iḍāfa* طرح ← جمع\زيادة\إضافة

١ أنتج	٢ سأل	٣ بالضبط
٤ تمهيدي	٥ خرْج	٦ ابتدأ
٧ شمال	٨ مذنب	٩ على الأكثر
١٠ معطي العون	١١ طقس رطب	١٢ شامل
١٣ أوّل	١٤ بالرغم من	١٥ يمينًا
١٦ متطرّفي	١٧ دائم	١٨ صديق

Exercise 4. Complete the sentence with an appropriate accusative expression:

e.g.: وقّع القائم بالأعمال ... سيادته.

← وقّع القائم بالأعمال نيابةً عن سيادته.

waqqa' al-qā'im bi-l-'a'māl niyābatan 'an siyādatihi.

١ اتّصلنا بهم على التلفون ... تأييدهم.
٢ تردّدنا في إرسال الشحن ... حجمه ووزنه.
٣ ... على هذه المعطيات نشكّ في ضبط الأرقام.
٤ درس القنصل المذكّرة ... قبل أن يقوم بكتابة الجواب.
٥ من أجل مثل هذه العملية الجراحية نعتمد على خبرته ... .
٦ كم ... ظلّوا ... نتيجة أبحاث المختبر؟
٧ شرح الخبير استعمال البرامج ... لم أستطع فهمه أبداً .
٨ تظاهر سكّان العاصمة ... على إلغاء الانتخابات.
٩ لنقدّم فهرس كبار مأمورينا ... رجاء قسم التشريفات.
١٠ كانوا يتكلّمون بصفتهم ... ولا ....

Exercise 5. (a) Write a notice for display on the factory notice-board. Head it with 'From/To/Date/Ref.' and mark it URGENT. State that owing to a fire in the electrical section, Workshop no. 3 will be closed for an unlimited time. Staff of Workshop no. 3 will be temporarily employed in other locations; details are in the annex. Sign the notice as Deputy Head of Production Dept.; mark a copy to Personnel and Safety Depts. and Supervisors of Workshops 1, 2 and 3.

(b) Write a further and similar notice, dated three weeks later, referring to (a) and stating that Workshop no. 3 is being reopened. Staff normally working there are to return to their usual workplace from next Saturday (give the time and date). Thank the staff for their cooperation.

Exercise 6. Replace the simple verb with a verb + verbal noun:

e.g.: جدّدوا المكتب. ← قاموا بتجديد المكتب.

qāmū bi-tajdīd al-maktab.

١ أُستبدل البرنامج مؤقّتاً تمهيداً لتوسيع القسم.

٢ مِن الممكن أن تُدرس المعطيات مدّةً طويلةً.
٣ حُلّت مشكلة البرمجة بمساعدة خبير من المكتب المركزي.
٤ إستلموا ثاني شحنٍ أمس.
٥ أُستلم ثاني شحن أمس.

Exercise 7. Renumber this partial list of contents with Arabic figures and symbols:

I مبادئ الإدارة المنتجة
1 بناء الإدارة
2 الربح والخسارة
3 الاستثمارات
(i) الاستثمار الرأسمالي
(ii) استثمارات طويلة الأجل
(iii) استثمارات قصيرة ومتوسطة الأجل
4 تمويل تكاليف التشغيل

Suggest titles for Chapters 5 (divided into two sections) and 6, and a general title for Part II of the document, all with appropriate numbering.

Exercise 8. Complete with an expression of circumstance:

e.g.: وصلوا ... ← وصلوا حاملين الوثائق.

waṣalū ḥāmilīn al-wathā'iq.

١ أخوه ... يعرف الإحصاءات معرفةً ممتازةً.
٢ خرجوا في الشارع ...
٣ أعدنا قراءة الأرقام ...
٤ كيف تمكننا الإجابة على هذا الطلب ...؟
٥ استنتج استنتاجًا غير صحيح و...
٦ قد اتّصل أمس ...
٧ لا يستطيع أحد أن يفهم تمامًا هذه النظرية، خاصّةً و...
٨ وقّع الوزير المذكّرة ...
٩ في نهاية خطابها أضافت الأستاذة ...
١٠ يجب أن تعيد دراسة كلّ النصّ، ...

Exercise 9. Here is part of the Chairman and Managing Director's Message heading the 2004 Annual Report of the Commercial Bank of Kuwait. Study it first, then read it aloud, then answer the questions:

موجز تقرير سنة ٢٠٠٤ للبنك التجاري الكويتي

ويسرّني أن أعلن بأن مجلس الإدارة قد أوصى(1) للجمعية(2) العامّة لمساهمي البنك بتوزيع أرباح نقدية بنسبة ٥٠٪ من القيمة الاسمية للأسهم المسجّلة في دفاتر البنك حتّى تاريخ انعقاد الجمعية العامّة.

ويتوجّب(3) علينا، أنا وزملائي أعضاء مجلس الإدارة، أن أتوجّه بالشكر الجزيل(4) لعملائنا(5) الكرام(6) لثقتهم(7) واختيارهم لمنتجات البنك التجاري الكويتي، ومن مساهمي البنك لدعمهم الأخ جمال المطوى *(jamāl al-muṭawa)* رئيس المدراء العامين ورئيس الجهاز التنفيذي.

كما أودّ(8) أن أتوجّه بالشكر والتقدير لرؤساء وأعضاء مجالس الإدارات السابقة لجهودهم الملموسة(9) في وضع أسس النجاحات المتتالية(10) الّتي حققها البنك خلال السنوات الماضية.

(1) أوصى بِ *'awṣa* IV *bi-* to recommend (2) جمعية (here:) meeting
(3) يتوجب *yatawajjab* V = يجب I (4) جزيل جزال *jazīl jizāl* abundant
(5) عميل عملاء *'amīl 'umalā'* client (6) كرام *kirām* = كرماء
(7) ثقة *thiqa* confidence, trust (8) ودّ يودّ *wadda yawaddu* I to want
(9) ملموس *malmūs* tangible
(10) متتال\المتتالي *mutatālin, al-mutatālī* (weak) successive

١ هل يعلن الخطاب خبراً طيّباً للمساهمين أم لا؟ اشرح التفاصيل.
٢ عند ذكر رئيس مجلس الإدارة للأرباح، كيف يتوجّه للعملاء؟
٣ ما هو رأيك عن الربح المذكور؟ عادى، فوق العادي؟
٤ يشير الرئيس إلى أعضاء مجالس الإدارات سابقة. ماذا يقول بخصوصهم؟
٥ الربح مؤسس على أيّة قيمة؟
٦ ما هو الجهاز التنفيذي؟ كيف يختلف من مجلس الإدارة؟
٧ اشرح عبارة "منتج" في القرينة المصرفية.
٨ اذكر أهمّ نقط المتعلّقة باقتصاد الكويت.

Exercise 10. Examine this table and answer the questions:

التوزيع النسبي لطلبة(1) التعليم العالي (٪) حسب التصنيف(2) الدولي لمستويات التعليم العالي، البلدان العربية وبلدان مقارنة: ١٩٩٩\٢٠٠٠

البلد(3)	أقل من الدرجة الجامعية الأولى	الدرجة الجامعية الأولى	الدرجة الجامعية العليا
الأردن	٨٣,٧٣	٢٠,٨٩	٠,٢٨
الإمارات	١٠٠,٠٠	٠,٠٠	٠,٠٠
البحرين	٩٤,٤٨	٥,٥٢	٠,٠٠
السعودية	٩٢,٨٠	٤,٦٧	٢,٥٣
الكويت	٩٨,٣٤	٠,٠٠	١,٦٦
المغرب	٩٢,٧٦	٢,٠٦	٥,١٩
اليمن	٨٥,٠٧	١٤,٩٢	٠,٠١
تونس	٨٣,٤٢	١٠,٨٤	٥,٧٤
جزر القمر(4)	٦٤,٢٩	٣٥,٧١	٠,٠٠
جيبوتي	٣١,٠٥	٦٨,٩٥	٠,٠٠
فلسطين	٩٢,٧٦	٧,٢٤	٠,٠٠
لبنان	٨٨,٨٣	١٠,٤٧	٠,٧٠
ليبيا	٦٤,٩٤	٣٢,٥٦	٢,٥٠
مصر	٩٤,٩٢	٤,٤٠	٠,٦٨
إسرائيل	٧٧,٧٥	١٩,٦٥	٢,٦٠
الصين	٥١,٧٧	٤٧,٤٩	٠,٧٣
كوريا الجنوبية	٥٨,٦٩	٤٠,٢٩	١,٠٢

(UNESCO Institute for Statistics [UIS]: Statistical Tables for Knowledge in Arab Countries, 2003)

(1) طلبة *ṭaliba* demand (2) تصنيف *taṣnīf* classification

(3) بلد بلاد (here:) country (4) جزر القمر *juzur al-qamar* Comores

١ قارن أرقام إسرائيل وفلسطين. ماذا هناك قابل للاهتمام؟

٢ ما رأيك عن أرقام الكويت؟ هل تستغرب منها؟

٣ اين توجد أعلى طلبة لتعليم الدرجة الجامعية الأولى؟

٤ جد بلدين عربيين بأرقام مقارنة واشرح اختلاف اقتصاديهما.

Key to exercises

NB.: The Arabic text is transcribed only selectively.

Chapter 1.

Ex. 1 1 *'idha kān mumaththilu l-'ummāl ḥāḍirīn li-l-mufāwaḍa fa-'inna ṭaraf al-'idāra ḥāḍir 'ayḍan.* 2 *'inna nkhifāḍ al-'intāj fi sh-sharq al-'awsaṭ huwa laysa as-sabab al-waḥīd li-rtifā' al-'as'ār al-'ālamīya.* 3 *'awwal nuqṭa 'ala barnāmaj al-ḥukūma l-ishtirākīya l-jadīda hiya stiqrār ziyādat ṣādirātina z-zirā'īya min 'ajl ta'yīd iqtiṣād al-bilād.* 4 *qad fāwaḍna mudda ṭawīla ḥatta al-wuṣūl 'ila muwāfaqa 'ala ta'wīḍ maqbūl li-l-'ummāl.* 5 *'innana narfiḍ tamāman sharḥahum li-'adam daf' hādha d-dayn li'annahum ya'rifūna bi-ḍ-ḍabṭ shurūṭ qurūḍ al-bank.* 6 *fīmā yata'allaq bi-tawqī' al-'aqd nufaḍḍil 'an tantaẓirū rujū' mudīr qism al-muḥāsabāt li-'anna jadwal al-istithmārāt al-muqtaraḥ mu'aqqad jiddan.* 7 *turīd ash-sharika taṭbīq shurūṭ daf' maqbūla li-jamī' zabā'īniha dūn 'ayy tamyīz bayn al-kibār wa-ṣ-ṣighār.* 8 *yaṭlub ra'īs al-handasa musā'adatana li-táswiyat khilāf ḥadath fi qismihi bayn thalātha 'ummāl an-nawba l-laylīya wa-mushrifihim.* 9 *'innana na'tabir 'anna l-iqtirāḥ 'ījābī wa-maqbūl wa-nanwī 'an naṭlub muwāfaqat al-mudīr al-'āmm khilāl al-ijtimā' al-muqbil.* 10 *nashkurukum 'ala ḥuḍūrikum fi l-mu'tamar al-'akhīr wa-khāṣṣatan 'ala qtirāḥātikum al-mufīda fi l-buḥūth al-mālīya.*

Ex. 2 1 ما هو رأي وزارة الداخلية في مطالب الولايات المتحدة؟

2 ان كل مستقبل حزبنا يتوقف على الانتخاب الإقليمية ،

3 إحدى مشاكلنا في تنمية القطاع الخاص في هذا البلاد هي عدم وجود نقل عام مناسب للعمال،

4 إن الضريبة تبلغ ٢٠٪ تقريبا من تكاليف إنتاجنا في هذا المصنع.

5 لو تمكّنّا من الرأسمال المناسب لاستطعنا أن نستفيد من هذه الفرصة الاستثمارية الممتازة.

6 تقدم المتظاهرون حتى ميدان البرلمان ولكنهم وقفوا وانسحبوا عندما لقوا الشرطة أمام بناية المجلس.

7 لا يوجد محلّ للناقلات الكبرى وصار ضروريا تمديد الميناء كله.

8 ترتفع أسعار المنتجات البترولية على السوق العالمية أسرع مما ينخفض مستوى إنتاج النفط الخام في أكثرية الحقول الهامّة.

9 كان بعض الطلاب غائبين عن الاجتماع الافتتاحي للكلية الهندسية.

10 لن تنحلّ مشاكل الشرق الأوسط إلّا إذا أخذت كل الأطراف بعين الاعتبار مصالح الفلسطينيين.

Chapter 2.

Ex. 1 1 خبّاز، خبازة 2 لحّام، لحام 3 بنّاء، بناء 4 برّاد، برادة
5 طبّاخ، طباخة 6 خيّاط(ة)، خياطة 7 جرّاح، جراحة 8 نقّاش، نقاشة
1 مطار 2 ملعب ملاعب 3 مكتب\مكتبة مكاتب 4 مطعم مطاعم
5 محطّة 6 مدرسة مدارس 7 مخرج مخارج 8 مصنع مصانع

Ex. 2 (possible answers:) 1 ستّة مدراء. المدير العامّ مسؤول عن إدارة الشركة كلّها. مدير الهندسة مسؤول عن العمليات الهندسية خارج الإنتاج، ومدير الإنتاج يهتمّ بالإنتاج. مدير المبيعات مسؤول عن بيع المنتجات، ومدير المالية مسؤول عن إدارة مال الشركة، بينما مدير شؤون الموظّين مسؤول عن إدارة الموظّفين.
2 رئيس الأمن مسؤول. هو يرفع تقريراً لمدير شؤون الموظّين.
3 ستّة رؤساء. 4 المستشار القانوني.

5 يقوم بالمفاوضة رئيس العلاقات الصناعية.
6 لمدير شؤون الموظّفين. 7 هو مسؤول أيضًا عن تخطيط المهن.
8 إنّ مسؤول يرفع تقريراً لرئيسه، والرئيس لمديره.
9 توجد أربعة مستويات استخدام في الجدول.
10 يجوز أن يهتمّ بدفع التعويض والأبدال ومدفوعات إضافية.
Ex. 3 1 الحفّار، مثقب 2 الطبّاخ، المطبخ، المطعم 3 المحطّات
4 المجلس 5 مبارد، برّادين 6 جرّاحون، المستشفى
Ex. 4 1 وصل 2 وقف 3 صنع 4 نسي 5 أخذ 6 قول 7 فيد 8 كشف

Chapter 3.
Ex. 1 1 الأخ 2 أبوه 3 أخي 4 أخوه 5 أبي 6 الأب 7 أبيهم 8 أخيك
9 أبيكم 10 أخيه
Ex. 2 1 صير 2 أخر 3 زوج 4 ضيف 5 ظهر 6 بدء 7 ثني 8 ألمان
9 وفق 10 أخذ 11 جمع 12 رسل
Ex. 3 1 خيّاط 2 مطبخ 3 روضة 4 ضمان اجتماعي 5 مقهى
6 المختار 7 القدس 8 مركز جماعي 9 زوج، زوجه 10 تسجيل
11 أمّها أو أبوها 12 إخوان

Chapter 4.
Ex. 1 1 أرباح نصف سنوية 2 جمعية ذات مال كثير
3 المعطيات غير المحضّرة 4 الاجتماع شبه الرسمي
5 بأسهم غير عادية 6 – 7 المواصلات اللاسلكية
8 فائدة قابل للدفع فوراً 9 – 10 الهيكل عديم الأساس القانوني
11 في الظروف غير المقبولة لنا 12 الترجمة العربية الفرنساوية
Ex. 2 1 الضرائب الّتي يمكن تقديرها بالضبط
2 فوائد ندفعها\يدفعونها سنويًا 3 مساهم ليس عنده فهم السوق
4 الأسهم الّتي اشتريتها قبل سنة
5 أرباح لم يقدّروها ولم يشرحوها في جريدة اليوم
Ex. 3 1 هي موريتانيا والمغرب والجزائر وتونس والجماهيرية
الليبية ومصر والسودان.

٢. شارك الرؤساء والمدراء العامّون للهيئات المينائية.

٣. بحثوا بصورة رئيسية برنامج عمل للاتّحاد لسنة ٢٠٠٥.

٤. استغرق ثلاثة أيّام.

٥. ... إسكندرية، طرابلس، تونس، الجزائر، الدار البيضاء

Chapter 5.

Ex. 1 ١. أكلتا عشاءهما. ٢. شربتا قهوتهما وخرجتا.
٣. لا تأكل البنتان في المدرسة. ٤. تأكلان دائمًا في المطعم.
٥. وصلت رسالتان إليكما. ٦. هل حضّرتا الشوربة؟
٧. ضعا الصحنين على الطاولة. ٨. وصلت رسالاتكما.
٩. وصلا لتناول غداءهما. ١٠. خذاهما من هناك.
تأكل (no. 4) and وصلت (6, 7) all head a verbal sentence with a noun
subject, and therefore remain singular.

Ex. 2 ١. إنّ البنات يذهبن ألى مدرستهنّ.
٢. خذن تفّاحكنّ\تفّاحاتكنّ معكنّ. ٣. تذهب البنات ألى مدرستهنّ.
٤. كنّ يلعبن مع أخواتهنّ. ٥. أكلن فطورهنّ في البستان.
٦. لا تنسين أن تأمرن الفواكه.

Ex. 3 1(a) شرب شايه. (b) شربت شايها. (c) شربوا شايهم.
2(a) اذكر اسمك على الورقة. (b) اذكري اسمك على الورقة.
(c) اذكروا أسماءكم على الورقة. 3(a) صحفي ذو خبرة ممتازة
(b) صحفيون ذوو خبرة ممتازة (c) صحفية ذات خبرة ممتازة
4(a) كيف جاوب على طلبك؟ (b) كيف جاوبت على طلبك؟
(c) كيف جاوبوا على طلبكم؟ 5(a) سافر إلى مصر ليزور صديقه.
(b) سافرت إلى مصر لتزور صديقتها.
(c) سافروا إلى مصر ليزوروا أصدقاءهم.
6(a) لم يقل إلاّ الحقّ. (b) لم تقل إلاّ الحقّ. (c) لم يقولوا إلاّ الحقّ.

Ex. 4 (possible answer:) أعلنت جديداً حكومة العراق مناقصة عامّة
لشراء كمّيات كبيرة من الأغذية مثل الأرزّ وطحين القمح. وقال
وزير التجارة أنّ تنفيذ الشراء سيكون حرّاً ومفتوحًا، دون أيّة سرّية
أو محاباة ولا كمى كانت العادة تحت الحكومة السابقة.

Chapter 6.

Ex. 1 1 .عولج\يعالج الطفل المريض *'ūlij, yu'ālaj*
2 .تُردِّد\يتردّد في تطبيق العلاج *turuddid, yutaraddad*
3 .أقترح\يُقترح عملية جراحية *uqtúriḥ, yuqtáraḥ*
4 .أشتري\يُشترى الدواء في الصيدلية *ushtúrī, yushtára*
5 .أنسحب\ينسحب من هذا الوضع *unsúḥib, yunsáḥab*
6 .أُعلنت\تعلن التفاصيل فوراً *'u'linat, tu'lan*
7 .فووضت\تفاوض الميزانية الصحّية *fūwiḍat, tufāwaḍ*
8 .بُحث\يبحث وضع المريض *buḥith, yubḥath*
9 .إنّ الطلبات رُفضت\تُرفض *rufiḍat, turfiḍ*
10 .إنّ الطلبين رُفضا\يُرفضان *rufiḍā, yurfiḍān*
Ex. 2 1 ... وُقّعت النشرة الطبّية *wuqqi'at*
2 ... تُفووض شروط *tufūwiḍ* 3 ... أُستغني عن *ustughnī 'an*
4 ... يُستعمل علاج *yustu'mil* 5 ... أنسحب من المنطقة *unsúḥib min*
6 ... قُرّر في الأخبار *qurrir* 7 ... أُكتشف الجرثوم *uktúshif*
8 ... طُبّقت إجراءات *ṭubbiqat*
9 ... لم يُستفد كثيراً من *lam yustafad kathīran min*
10 ... يؤكّد في صحافة اليوم *yu'akkad*
Ex. 3 (possible answers:) 1 .أنّ المريض يتحسّن ...
2 .حقيقة ما قالوا. 3 ... كيف يتطوّر الوضع الاقتصادي ...
4 ... بُحث في الاجتماع ... 5 سُلّم تقرير طويل ...
6 .تُردّد ... 8 ...ارتفاع صادراتنا الزراعية. 7 ...أجنبي في البلدية
Ex. 4 (possible answers:) 1 أُكّدت\تؤكّد *'ukkidat, tu'akkad*
2 ووفق\يوافق *wūfiq, yuwāfaq* 3 أُستعملت\تُستعمل *ustu'milat, tusta'mal* 4 أُعلن\يعلن *'u'lin, yu'lan* 5 وُقّعت\تُوقّع *wuqqi'at, tuwaqqa'* 6 أُحتجّ \ يُحتجّ *uḥtujj, yuḥtajj* 7 ذُكرت\تُذكر *dhukirat, tudhkar* 8 طُبّقت\تُطبّق *ṭubbiqat, tuṭabbaq* 9 حوول\يحاول *ḥūwil, yuḥāwal* 10 وُجدت\توجد *wujidat, tūjad*

Chapter 7.

Ex. 1 1 نتلفز *nutalfiz* 2 تصدر *tuṣdir* 3 يبرهن *yubarhin*
4 يُتّهم *yuttaham* 5 يتلفن *yutalfin*

Ex. 2 (possible answers:) 1 عند دعوى مدني تحكم شكوة بين
طرفين ولكن في دعوى جنائي تحكم جريمة.
2 ضرر ماديّ مثلاً 3 يقول الشاهد ما يعرف شخصيًا عن الموضوع.
4 أنّ الحكاية صحيحة ومعروفة أيضًا عند الجميع. 5 القتل
6 يكذب 7 لأنّ الحقيقة ضرورية من أجل حكم عدل.
8 تكليف استبدال البضائع
9 استخدام مترجم مقبول عند الطرفين وعند القاضي
10. لا؛ يجب مثلاً اعتبار غرض القول: لماذا نشره المدّعى عليه؟

Ex. 3 1 قرّ 2 فلسف 3 ذنب 4 دعو 5 زور 6 أخر 7 أمريكا
8 شفي 9, 10 ثني 11 رجع 12 ترجم

Ex. 4 1 لا. يجب على المدّعي أن يثبت أنّ المتّهم مذنب.
2 لا يمكن اليوم إدانة شخص بسبب القذف مثلاً على أساس أنّ
القذف كان جريمةً في الماضي، أو أنّه سيكون جريمةً في المستقبل.
3 لا شكّ أنّ توجد حالات خلاف بين مبادئ الإعلان وقوانين وطنية،
خاصّةً في التفاصيل وفي التطبيق.

Chapter 8.

Ex. 1 1 أخًا أصغر 2 أخاه الأصغر 3 زميلين سابقين
4 اقتراحات أخرى 5 زملاء أجانب 6 مبدءاً واحداً 7 تقارير ورسالات
8 أب 9 خبزاً وملحًا وزبدةً وفواكه 10 دوراً أساسيًا

Ex. 2 1 إمرأة 2 جمهورية 3 بعيد عن 4 بدأ 5 ربح 6 لاإنساني
7 سالم 8 وظّف\توظيف\استخدم\استخدام 9 الحقّ علينا
10 نظيف\نظّف 11 بالضبط 12 يكذب

Ex. 3 1 رجع 2 رجو 3 جري 4 جرح 5 حلّ 6 زور 7 نوم 8 نمو
9 دحرج 10 وحد 11 ترجم 12 يابان

Ex. 4 1 درسنا شهادة التاجر. 2 رفضنا شهادة التاجر.
3 سجّلنا شهادة التاجر. 4 كتبنا شهادة التاجر.

5 أضرب السبّاكون لعدم تعويض تكاليفهم.
6 أضرب العمّال لعدم تعويض تكاليفهم.
7 أضرب الزملاء لعدم تعويض تكاليفهم.
8 أضرب المحامون لعدم تعويض تكاليفهم.
9 عالج الطبيب البنت بواسطة دواء جديد.
10 ساعد الطبيب البنت بواسطة دواء جديد.
11 ساعد الطبيب البنت بواسطة علاج جديد.
12 ساعدت الممرّضة البنت بواسطة علاج جديد.
13 للفطور يتناول الضيوف عادةً فواكه وقهوةً.
14 للفطور يتناول الضيوف دائمًا فواكه وقهوةً.
15 للغداء يتناول الضيوف دائمًا فواكه وقهوةً.
16 للغداء يتناول الضيوف دائمًا فواكه وعصيراً.
17 للغداء يتناول الضيوف دائمًا فواكه ولبنًا.
18 للغداء تتناول أمّي دائمًا فواكه ولبنًا.
19 للغداء تتناول أمّي كلّ يوم فواكه ولبنًا.
20 للغداء تأمر أمّي كلّ يوم فواكه ولبنًا.
21 إنّ سكّان القرية جلسوا في البلدية من أجل بحث هامّ.
22 إنّ شيوخ القرية جلسوا في البلدية من أجل بحث هامّ.
23 إنّ شيوخ القرية جلسوا في المكتب من أجل بحث هامّ.
24 (possible answer:) إنّ نسوان القرية جلسن في المكتب من أجل بحث هامّ.

Ex. 5 1 تأخّرا لأنّهما زارا صديقهما\تأخّرتا لأنّهما زارتا صديقهما\تأخّرن لأنّهنّ زرن صديقهنّ في المستشفى العامّ.
2 احتجّا على قولهما\احتجّتا على قولهما\احتججن على قولهنّ.
3 يهتمّان بأطفالهما\تهتمّان بأطفالهما\يهتممن بأطفالهنّ.
4 يريدان أن يساعداهما\تريدان أن تساعداهما\ يردن أن يساعدنهنّ.
5 كانا شاهدين في المحكمة\كانتا شاهدتين في المحكمة\ كنّ شاهدات في المحكمة.
6 طلبا مساعدة أصداقائهما الأقرب في وضعهما الصعب\

طلبتا مساعدة أصداقائهما الأقرب في وضعهما الصعب\
طلبن مساعدة أصداقائهنّ الأقرب في وضعهنّ الصعب.
7 يستعملان معرفتهما للغة العربية في شغلهما الفنّي\
تستعملان معرفتهما للغة العربية في شغلهما الفنّي\
يستعملن معرفتهنّ للغة العربية في شغلهنّ الفنّي.
8 لا تنسيا أن تذكرا اسميكما عندما تطلبان الكتب المحجوزة لكما\
لا تنسيا أن تذكرا اسميكما عندما تطلبان الكتب المحجوزة لكما\
لا تنسين أن تذكرن أسماءكنّ عندما تطلبن الكتب المحجوزة لكنّ.
9 هذان هما الطبيبان اللذان يستطيعان أن يساعداهما\
هاتان هما الطبيبتان اللتان تستطيعان أن تساعداهما\
هؤلاء هنّ الطبيبات اللواتي يستطعن أن يساعدنهنّ.
10 أنّ الشاهدين حاولا أن يكذبا في حكايتهما\
أنّ الشاهدتين حاولتا أن تكذبا في حكايتهما\
أنّ الشاهدات حاولن أن يكذبن في حكايتهنّ.

Ex. 6 (possible answers:) 1 .تغيّر الحكومة بانقلاب ولا بالانتخاب
2 .إنّنا ندفع أكثر للعمّال المؤهلين بسبب تخصّصهم
3 .إذا كنت مريضًا يجب أن تستوصف طبيبًا
4 .الممرّضة تساعد الطبيب بعلاج المرضى
5 .لا يمكن المدير أن يدير الشركة إلاّ بتأييد الموظّفين جميعهم
6 .بعد سنتي الخسارة بدأت الشركة أن تربح من عملياتها التجارية
7 في المفاوضة المنتجة عند الطرفين الحقّ في التكلّم الحرّ من أجل تسوية دائمة للخلاف.
8 .ترجم هذه الرسالة من العربية إلى الألمانية لو سمحت
9 .كنت مريضًا وناديت الطبيب فوراً
10 .يمكننا أن نقول أنّ القلب هو طلمبة الجسم
11 .يقرأون اللغة العربية ولكنهم لا يكتبونها بالضبط
12 .في الساعة السادسة ينظرون إلى الأخبار على التلفزة

Ex. 7 1 مبرهن، مبرهن عليه، برهان *mubarhin, mubarhan ʿalayhi, burhān*

2 مستوصف، مستوصف، استيصاف *mustawṣif, mustawṣaf, istīṣāf*
3 كائن، –، كون *kā'in, –, kawn*
4 معتمد، معتمد عليه، اعتماد *mu'támid, mu'támad 'alayhi, i'timād*
5 معلن، معلن، إعلان *mu'lin, mu'lan, 'i'lān*
6 مرخّص، مرخّص، ترخيص *murakhkhiṣ, murakhkhaṣ, tarkhīṣ*
7 ناو\الناوي، منويّ، نية *nāwin (an-nāwī), manwīy, niya*
8 مصدر، مصدر، إصدار *muṣdir, muṣdar, 'iṣdār*
9 متناول، متناول، تناول *mutanāwil, mutanāwal, tanāwul*
10 مستقبل، مستقبل، استقبال *mustaqbil, mustaqbal, istiqbāl*
11 قارئ، مقروء. قراءة *qāri', maqrū', qirā'a*
12 متقاعد، –، تقاعد *mutaqā'id, –, taqā'ud*

Ex. 8 (possible answers:) 1 فشلت كلّ جهودها في حلّ المشكلة.
2 جميع أبنائها متزوّجون بنسوان من القرية.
3 إن الشباب المدّعى عليهم غير مذنبين بالفعل.
4 في المستشفى يتخصّص كثير من الجراحين في أمراض الأطفال.
5 أبو صديقي مأمور وأمّه معلّمة في نفس المدرسة.
6 بعد الإصلاح الاجتماعي تركّزت الوزارة أكثر في التدريب المهني للبنات.
7 لا تنس أهمّية التغييرات الاجتماعية الّتي حدثت أخيراً.
8 يهتمّ الكاتب ببرنامج اجتماعات مجلس الإدارة.
9 كان عنوان محاضرته "الوضع السياسي لليهود في فلسطين".
10 خسارتنا الفعلية محدودة إذا أخذنا بعين الاعتبار التعويض.
11 كانوا جميعهم إخوان في نفس النقابة.
12 إنّ القضية قابلة لاهتمامنا الخاصّ.

Ex. 9 1 صحيح *ṣaḥīḥ* 2 جهد *juhd* 3 يحكم *yaḥkum*
4 يخسر *yakhsar* 5 يمنح *yamnaḥ* 6 شيخ *shaykh* 7 فقير *faqīr*
8 يبرهن *yubarhin* 9 يعزل *ya'zil* 10 مثقب *mithqab* 11 يستقيل *yastaqīl*
12 نظام *niẓām*

Ex. 10 1 حُكم عليهم 2 عولج 3 تُضَرّ 4 تُرجم 5 يُسرق
6 تُنوولت 7 أُتّهم 8 تُلفز أمس

Ex. 11 (possible answers:) 1 شُرح، يُشرح 2 شُكّ، يُشكّ
3 قيم، يقام 6 أُحتجّ، يُحتجّ 5 سُجّل، يسجّل 4 كُتب\يُكتب
Ex. 12 1 الموظّفون الكبار 2 شخص ليس عنده فهم الأمر
3 النصّ المكتوب باللغتين العربية والألمانية
4 النتائج الّتي لا يستطيع أحد شرحها
5 سياسات أحزاب مختلفة 6 التقرير الّذي يصدروه مرّتين بالسنة
7 فشل البرنامج لأنّ الاستثمار لم يكف.

Chapter 9.

Ex. 1 1 تنازلاً واسعًا 3 رفضًا شديداً 2 مرضًا خطراً
4 كلّ الشرح 7 تأمينًا تامّاً 6 معرفةً خبير 5 تصادمًا خفيفًا
8 جواب طفل\جوابًا طفليًا
Ex. 2 1 تمهيداً ل\عملاً ب\بناءً على\وفقًا ل
2 نظراً إلى\عملاً ب\بناءً على\وفقًا ل 3 نيابةً عن\تأييداً ل
4 تأييداً ل\إكرامًا ل 7 خوفًا على 6 إكرامًا لك 5 خوفًا من
8 رغبةً في\أجابةً ل
Ex. 3 1 نائب مدير 4 مساعدين فنّيين 3 خبراء 2 سمساراً
5 حفّاراً 6 زملاءك
Ex. 5 1 سألونا إيّاها. 3 سنريهم إيّاها. 2 أعطاني إيّاه.
4 لم يمنحهم إيّاه. 5 لم يعطوه إيّاه.
Ex. 6 1 هل تجده زميلاً طيّبًا؟ 2 أعتبرها بنتًا لطيفةً.
3 ... وأعتبره أنا غير كاف. 4 انّنا نعتبر التعويض كافيًا،
5 لم يعتبروه أهمّ مشكلة. 6 كيف تجد العقد؟ - معقّداً.
Ex. 7 (possible answers:) 1 وكيل بائع أو مشتر
2 تأمين ضدّ كلّ الأخطار 3 دفع على خسارة
4 شخص يستلم التعويض 6 مالك البيت 5 لا مؤمّن ولا مؤمّن عليه
7 الّذي يدفع الأجر ألى صاحب البيت 8 ثمن يدفعه المؤمّن عليه
Ex. 8 مطار، طيران، يطير. وقّع، موقع، توقيع. سنة، سنويًا.
قاض، قضية. صادرات، إصدار. حرائق، احترق، أحرق.
تعقيد، معقّد، عقود. أفاد، فائدة، استفاد، يفيد. قد.

Chapter 10.

Ex. 1 1 .سنقوم بتجديد البناية كلّها
2 .قام الملحق بتسليم تقريره السرّي
3 .قمنا بتطبيق أنظمة القانون التجاري
4 .يقوم السفير بدراسة المذكّرة الآن
5 .إنّهما قاما بافتتاح العلاقات الدبلوماسية
6 .قمنا باتّخاذ هذه الإجراءات في مصالح اللاجئين
7 .سيقوم ناطق بلساننا بتقديم اقتراحنا أمام الجلسة المقبلة
8 .تقوم القنصلية بإصدار الفيزات الإكرامية لكبار المأمورين فقط

Ex. 2 1 .تمّ تطبيق نفس الأنظمة 2 .تمّ اتّخاذ الإجراءات المناسبة
3 .تمّ احتلال المدينة كلّها 4 .يجري بحث نفس الأنظمة
5 .تمّ انسحاب من المناطق المحتلّة
6 .تمّ توقيع المذكّرة فوراً 7 .تمّ وفاق\تمّت موافقة على البند الثالث
8 ؟متى سيتمّ إرسال المذكّرة

Ex. 3 1 .لن يحضر حضراتهم 2 .سيحضر سيادة الوزير الحفلة
3 ؟أين تسكن حضرتها 4 .نشكرك يا سيادة القاضي
5 .أرجوك قلبيًا يا أستاذ
6 .تفضّل بقبول هذا ، سيادة المدير

Ex. 4 1 .لم يفاوضوا أيّ تعويض 2 .شرحنا سياستنا
3 .قدّم السفير احتجاجنا 4 .سنجاوب على طلبهم
5 .بعد دراسة قضية اللاجئين منحنا اللجوء
6 .إنّ القنصلية تصدر وتجدّد جوازات السفر صباحًا

Ex. 5 (possible answer:) قام رئيس جنوب أفريقيا بزيارة السودان استغرقت ثلاثة أيّام. زار منطقة دارفور وبحث مع رئيس السودان عمر البشير الوضع في هذا الإقليم بعد ٢٢ شهراً من الحرب. وقد شارك السيد مبيكي أيضًا في الاحتفال المتعلّق بذكرى ٤٩ سنة من استقلال السودان.

Ex. 7 1 .بُحث الشروط يومين *(buḥith)*
2 .نُشر نصّ منح الحصانة *(nushir)*
3 .وُصل إلى وضع مشترك بين الطرفين *(wuṣil)*

4 أُستلمِ خبر سرّي وشفري. *(ustulim)*
5 يُحضَّر نصّ البنود. *(yuḥaḍḍar)*
6 مُنح الحكم الذاتي بعد مفاوضات ثنائية طويلة وصعبة. *(munih)*

Chapter 11.

Ex. 1 1 زعماء رجعيون السياسة 2 زعيم رجعي السياسة
3 في ثورة شعبية الأساس 4 اسم ملك مطلق السلطة
5 مدّة كبيرة التغييرات 6 نائب شيوعي راديكالي الأفكار
7 قرون كبيرة التغييرات 8 قرن كبير التغييرات
9 اتّخاذ إجراء إيجابي النتيجة 10 إجراء إيجابي النتيجة
1 الزعماء الرجعيون السياسة 2 الزعيم الرجعي السياسة
3 في الثورة الشعبية الأساس 4 اسم الملك المطلق السلطة
5 المدّة الكبيرة التغييرات 6 النائب الشيوعي الراديكالي الأفكار
7 القرون الكبيرة التغييرات 8 القرن الكبير التغييرات
9 اتّخاذ الإجراء الإيجابي النتيجة 10 الإجراء الإيجابي النتيجة
Ex. 2 1 زعماء ذوو سياسة رجعية 2 زعيم ذو سياسة رجعية
3 في ثورة ذات أساس شعبي 4 اسم ملك ذي سلطة مطلقة
5 مدّة ذات تغييرات كبيرة 6 نائب شيوعي ذو أفكار راديكالية
7 قرون ذات تغييرات كبيرة 8 قرن ذو تغييرات كبيرة
9 اتّخاذ إجراء ذي نتيجة إيجابية 10 إجراء ذو نتيجة إيجابية
1 الزعماء ذوو السياسة الرجعية 2 الزعيم ذو السياسة الرجعية
3 في الثورة ذات الأساس الشعبي 4 اسم الملك ذي السلطة المطلقة
5 النائب الشيوعي ذو الأفكار الراديكالية
6 القرن ذو التغييرات الكبيرة 7 المدّة ذات التغييرات الكبيرة
8 الإجراء ذو النتيجة الإيجابية 9 القرون ذات التغييرات الكبيرة
10 اتّخاذ الإجراء ذي النتيجة الإيجابية
Ex. 3 1 حركة مقاومة قليلة الأعضاء 2 الحركة الغالية البرنامج
3 ثورة تامّة النجاح 4 بضائع مرتفعة الأسعار
5 شعب طويل التاريخ 6 الزعماء الواضحون الغرض
7 طلمبة كبيرة القوة 8 قوة الناس الكثار المال

Ex. 4 7 + 2, 5, 6; 8 + 4, 5; 9 + 1, 4, 5; 10 + 1, 5; 11 + 1, 5; 12 + 3

Ex. 5 (possible answers:) 1 ... تداخل الحزب الوطني. 2 ... تغيّر تاريخ أوروبّا تمامًا. 3 ... عاصمة فلسطين. 4 ... صارت مستقلّةً كثير من الدول النامية. 5 ... أنّ الأولى تتركّز في الاستقرار بينما الثانية تتركّز في الإصلاح. 6 ... لأنّهم اعتبروه ضدّ مصالح العمّال. 7 ... الاعتقاد بحقّ في تأسيس وطن يهودي على أرض فلسطين. 8 يعتبر كثير من السياسيين أنّ أحسن فرصة للسلام هي ... 9 ... الإسلام والمسيحية واليهودية. 10 ... تسوية الخلاف العربي الإسرائيلي على أساس عدل.

Ex. 6 1 تسكن أكثريتهم في تركيا وأصغر عددهم في العراق. 2 وضع الأكراد العراقيين أحسن منه في تركيا وإيران، 3 تركيا. وخاصّة فيما يتعلّق بعدم التمييز من قبل الحكومة. 4 أقلّيات أخرى قابلة للذكر: السنّيون والمسيحيون واليهود.

Chapter 12.

Ex. 1 1 رفضت اللجنة الضمان المقترح مراجعةً جميع الشروط. 2 غيّروا شروط القرض مخفّضين الفائدة السنوية بـ ٥،٠٪. 3 ساعدت الحكومة الجديدة اقتصاد البلاد مؤيّدةً القطاع الخاصّ. 4 يلعب البنك دوراً هامّاً مقدّمًا قروض واطئة الفائدة للفلاّحين. 5 ترك الوفد البلاد راجعًا إلى باريس.

Ex. 2 1 خفّضنا الخرج نتركّز في التدريب أثناء العمل. 2 أعلنت الحكومة حالة الطوارئ تطلب العون الدولي. 3 أعدنا تخطيط قطاع النقل نمدد البنية التحتية المتعلّقة به. 4 نؤيّد تصنيع البلاد نزيد الضرائب على المستوردات. 5 بدأوا البحث يسألون رأينا بخصوص تنفيذ العون الغذائي.

Ex. 3 1 سأل الرئيس الخبراء وليس مؤهّلاً في الاقتصاد. 2 كيف يمكننا أن نفاوض وليست عندنا بضائع قابلة للبيع؟ 3 لا نستطيع قبول قروض جديدة ووضع اقتصادنا ضعيف.

4 أعدنا إنجاز المشروع وقد انحلّت المشكلة المالية.
5 قاموا بإنجاز البرنامج وهم على علم بعدم استقرار القطاع.
Ex. 4 (possible answers:) 1 رفضت اللجنة الضمان المقترح مغيّرةً كلّ الأرقام.
2 غيّروا شروط القرض يضيفون مواداً أشدّ.
3 ساعدت الحكومة الجديدة اقتصاد البلاد تخفّض الضرائب.
4 يلعب البنك دوراً هامّاً يؤيّد القطاع الزراعي.
5 ترك الوفد البلاد وليس ناجحًا في غرضه.
1 خفّضنا الخرج ونحن نستبدل الآلات القديمة.
2 أعلنت الحكومة حالة الطوارئ تنادي مساعدة الجيش.
3 أعدنا تخطيط قطاع النقل متركّزين في النقل النهري.
4 نؤيّد تصنيع البلاد ونحن نهتمّ بالتدريب المهني.
5 بدأوا البحث وليست عندنا الوثائق الأخيرة.
1 سأل الرئيس الخبراء وهو يعرف الموضوع أحسن منهم.
2 كيف يمكننا أن نفاوض ولا نصدّق أرقامهم؟
3 لا نستطيع قبول قروض جديدة ولم ندفع القرض الآخر.
4 أعدنا إنجاز المشروع متوجّهًا أوّلاً إلى مشاكل التمويل.
5 قاموا بإنجاز البرنامج عارفين عدم التمويل الكافي.
Ex. 5 1 أعادوا استكشاف المنطقة. 2 إعادة استكشاف المنطقة
3 إعادة توزيع العون الغذائي 4 أعدنا إنجاز المشاريع الريفية.
5 أعادوا ذكر الموضوع 6 أعدنا استئجار شاحنات الوكالة.
7 إعادة ذكر الموضوع 8 إعادة إنشاء اقتصاد البلاد
Ex. 6 1 لا نستطيع المساعدة ولم توافق السلطات المحلّية.
2 كتبوا تقريراً مقترحين فيه مراجعة البنية التحتية كلّها.
3 لا تنجح جهود السكّان ولم يساعدهم الصندوق.
4 اقترضنا مبلغًا كبيراً ضمنّا تسديده والشروط طويلة الأجل.
5 وقعنا العقد وهو يطلب نسخةً من أجل مديره.
Ex. 7 1 اقترحوا شروطًا رفضناها بعد استشار خبرائنا.
2 ساعدنا البنك الدولي بتمديد قروضنا الثلاثة الطويلة الأجل.
3 تحاول الحكومة تجديد الاقتصاد وخاصّةً بإعادة إنشاء قطاع

الصادرات.

4 نفضّل التدريب أثناء العمل لأنّه أسهل وأرخص وأسرع.

5 أيّدهم البنك بواسطة (منح) قرض خاصٍ منخفض الفائدة.

Ex. 8 1 تأسّس في السنة ١٩٧٣ وفقًا لقرار القمّة العربية.

2 هو مؤسّسة دولية مستقلّة بالشخصية القانونية الدولية الكاملة.

3 أولاً المشاركة في تمويل المشاريع في أفريقيا؛ ثانيًا تشجيع مشاركة مصادر مالية عربية أخرى لنفس الغرض؛ وثالثاً المشاركة في عمليات العون الفنّي في المنطقة المذكورة.

4 يعمل في البلدان الأفريقية غير العربية.

5 علاقته مؤسّسة على مبدأ المساواة والصداقة.

- †تأسّس ≈ (is presumably) *ta'assas*, past tense of تأسّس *ta'assasa* V; we know أساس 'basis'; تأسّس ≈ 'was founded, established'. (NB: تأسّس cannot be read as a fem. sing. present of Form II; that would be تؤسّس *tu'assis*.)
- †(بالـ)شخصية *(bi-sh-)shakhṣīya* ≈ abstract noun of شخص 'person'; شخصية ≈ 'personality, identity'.
- †يُعدّ ≈ *yu'add*, present passive of verb عدّ I; we know noun عدد 'number'; يُعدّ ≈ 'is counted'.
- †استجابة ≈ *istijāba*, vb. noun of Form X hollow verb with root جوب or جيب; we know جاوب III 'to answer'; استجابةً ل ≈ *istijābatan li-* 'as an intended/positive response to'. (NB: the root is indeed جوب; root جيب exists, but not as a verb.)
- †تضامن ≈ *taḍāmun*, Form VI vb. noun from root ضمن; we know ضمان 'guarantee'; للتضامن ≈ 'for mutual guarantee, for solidarity'.
- †صداقة ≈ *ṣadāqa*, judging from the context an abstract noun; we know صديق 'friend'; صداقة ≈ 'friendship'. (NB: another vowelling, in this case wrong, might have been *[ṣidāqa]*.)
- †إسهام ≈ *'is-hām*, Form IV vb. noun from root سهم ; we know nouns سهم 'share' and مساهم 'shareholder'; الإسهام ≈ 'making

(someone) share'.

Chapter 13.

Ex. 1 1 استكشاف الفضاء لا يستغرب أحد منه في الوقت الحاضر. 2 النيل العظيم قد كتب كتّاب مختلفون عنه.
3 الثلج لا يخاف الأطفال منه أبداً.
4 الثلج لا يخافونه أبداً ويلعبون فيه.
5 تركيا وإيران هل يعرفهما مديرك؟
6 أكبر صاروخ قد أرسله الأمريكيون إلى القمر أمس.
7 البحر الأحمر قرأنا جميعنا عنه في دراستنا للتاريخ القديم.
8 كان الطقس رطبًا جداً والشمس لم نراها إلاّ قليلاً.
9 الوضع السياسي في الشرق الأقصى لا نفهمه جيّداً.
10 الأقمار الصناعية لا يعرف أحد عددها الدائر(ة) حول الدنيا حاليًا.

Ex. 2 1 لنتّصل\لتتّصل\ليتّصلوا فيهم
2 لنجاوب، لتجاوب، ليجاوبوا
3 لننتظر، لتنتظر، لينتظروا
4 لنستجوب\لتستجوب\ليستجوبوا الشاهد
5 لنقل\لتقل\ليقولوا الحقيقة
6 لنبق\لتبق\ليبقوا هنا
1 لا نتّصل\لا تتّصل\لا يتّصلوا فيهم
2 لا نجاوب، لا تجاوب، لا يجاوبوا
3 لا ننتظر، لا تنتظر، لا ينتظروا
4 لا نستجوب\لا تستجوب\لا يستجوبوا الشاهد
5 لا نقل\لا تقل\لا يقولوا الحقيقة
6 لا نبق\لا تبق\لا يبقوا هنا

Ex. 3 1 نفهم جميعنا أهمّية المطر من أجل القطاع الزراعي.
2 نشكّ في حقيقة حكاية الشاهد شكّاً عميقًا
3 لن ننسى أبداً النيل العظيم.
4 رئيت المحيط الهندي لأوّل مرّة وأنا ولد صغير.

5 هل تعرف منطقة الخليج العربي؟
6 قد وضع الأمين نقطتين على جدول أعمال اليوم.
Ex. 4 1 لو لم تمطر السماء. 2 لو كان السلام في المنطقة.
3 لو لم يكذبوا. 4 لو صار الطقس أحسن.
5 لو لم أنس اسم وعنوانهم. 6 لو انتظروا أكثر.
Ex. 5 The original title is الثلوج تغطي مرتفعات الإمارات

- †دون : we know دون 'without'; from the context دون ≈ 'below'.
- †ليل ≈ *layl*; we know ليلة 'night'; from the context ليل also ≈ 'night' (more exactly, 'nighttime').
- †خصوصاً ≈ *khuṣūṣan*; we know خاصّ 'special' and بخصوص 'concerning"; خصوصاً ≈ adverb '(e)specially, particularly'.
- †يبعد ≈ present tense of a Form I verb with root بعد; we know بعيد عن 'far from'; يبعد ≈ 'is distant' (the verb is in fact بعد يبعد (عن) *ba'uda yab'udu* I *('an)* 'to be distant (from)').

Chapter 14.

Ex. 1 1 غاب اليوم سيادة السفير.
2 كان احتجاجهم شديداً اللهجة.
3 في الماضي كان التجّار يسافرون راكبين الإبل.
4 دخلت الشرطة البيت وهم يحملون أسلحةً خفيفةً.
5 تنازل المؤمّن عليه عن التعويض وفقًا للمادّة الثالثة.
6 لا يفيدنا كثيراً أنّه يشرح العملية شرحًا طويلاً فنّيًا.
7 لا يمكنك إلغاء العقد والمفاوضات جارية.
8 كان يجب أن يوقفوا البحوث نظراً لغيبة الوزير.
9 قد أطلقوا أمس صاروخًا عظيمًا القوة تمهيداً لطيران إلى القمر.
10 إنّنا ننصح لكم بهذا العمل بصفتنا محاميكم.
11 ألقى وزير المالية خطابه ونصف النوّاب الحاضرين نائمون.
12 يجب أن ندرس الاتّهام دراسةً كاملةً.

Accusative forms: 1 اليوم time expression with no preposition.
2 شديداً predicate of كان, qualifying احتجاجهم with improper

agreement.
3 راكبين acc. of circumstance; الإبل direct object of راكبين .
4 البيت direct object of دخلت; أسلحةً خفيفةً direct object of يحملون
5 وفقًا ل adverbial phrase
6 كثيراً adverb; العملية direct object of يشرح ; شرحًا طويلاً فنّيًا absolute object of يشرح .
8 البحوث direct object of يوقفوا ; نظراً ل adverbial phrase.
9 صاروخًا direct object of أطلقوا ; عظيمًا qualifying صاروخًا with improper agreement; تمهيداً ل adverbial phrase.
10 محاميكم 'as' expression. 11 خطابه direct object of ألقى
12 الاتّهام direct object of ندرس ; دراسةً كاملةً absolute object of ندرس.

Ex. 2 1 ل 2 إكرامًا ل 2 عملاً ب\بناءً على 3 وفقًا ل\خوفًا من
4 تأييداً ل 8 تمهيداً ل 7 نظراً إلى 6 نيابةً عن 5 خوفًا على
(possible substitutions:) 1 رأي المساهمين 2 الملحق الجديد
3 وضع ممثّليهم 6 جميع زملائه 5 نجاح البرنامج 4 الإضراب العامّ
7 احتجاج صغار موظّفيهم 8 الإعلان العامّ

Ex. 3 1 ما أشدّه إفادةً. 3 ما أبسط النموذج. 2 ما أقواه.
4 ما أكبر أطفاله. 5 ما أطول هذه القضية.
6 كم نقوداً\من النقود خسرنا.

Ex. 4 1 قامت الوكالة بإعطاء عون الطوارئ.
2 جرى تفتيش المثقب عندما انفجرت البئر.
3 قاموا بتنفيذ الجزء الآخر من البرنامج قبل ابتداء الأمطار.
4 تقوم هذه الشركة بصورة رئيسية بتأمين حالات الكوارث الطبيعية.
5 لم يتمّ توقيع الاتّفاقية إلاّ بعد بحوث طويلة ومعقّدة.
6 يقوم الفدائيون بمقاومة قوات احتلال أرضهم.

Ex. 5 1 يا 2 يا 3 يا متخرّجات ومتخرّجين الكلّية 4 أيّها 5 يا

Ex. 6 (a)

البلاد: ....الأردنّ............ | الدستور: .مملكة دستورية........

المساحة: ..٨٩،٠٠٠...كم٢ | عدد السكّان: ..٥ ملايين.......

اللغات: .عربية (إنجليزية)....... | الأديان: إسلام ٩٦٪، م. ٤٪..

سنة الاستقلال: .١٩٤٦.. | العيد الوطني: ...٢٥ أيّار.....

عضوية منظّمات دولية رئيسية: .أمم المتّحدة (وكالات مختلفة)، المصرف العربي للتنمية.في أفريقيا، بنك عربي للتنمية، البنك الإسلامي وغيرها

الوحدة النقدية: .دينار (JD). | قيمتها: ..٠،٧\$، ..٠،٩\€

العاصمة: .عمّان.... | عدد سكّان العاصمة: ...١،٣ مليون......

المدن الرئيسية الأخرى: الزرقاء، معان، إربد، الكرك، مادابا، العقبة....

الموانئ الرئيسية: ..العقبة..............................

المنتجات المعدنية\الأولية: .الفوسفات، البوتاش، الزيت الصخري......

المنتجات الصناعية: .الأسمدة، موادّ للبناء..............

المنتجات الزراعية: .الخضر والفواكه (من وادي الأردنّ)............

قطاع الخدمات: .السياحة، النقل، المواصلات..........

(b)

البلاد: .الإمارات العربية المتّحدة.. | الدستور: .اتّحاد ٧ إمارات.....

المساحة: ..٨٣،٠٠٠.. كم٢ | عدد السكّان: .٣ ملايين تقريبًا..

اللغات: .عربية (فارسية، إنجليزية). | الأديان: إسلام ٩٦٪، غيرها ٤٪

سنة الاستقلال: .١٩٧١. | العيد الوطني: ..٢ ديسمبر.....

عضوية منظّمات دولية رئيسية: .أمم المتّحدة (وكالات مختلفة)، المصرف العربي للتنمية.في أفريقيا، أوبيك، صندوق النقد الدولي وغيرها

الوحدة النقدية: .درهم (AED). | قيمتها: ..٣،٧\$، ..٤،٨\€

العاصمة: .أبو ظبي... | عدد سكّان العاصمة: .٩٣٠،٠٠٠......

المدن الرئيسية الأخرى: .دبيّ، الفجيرة، الشارقة، رأس الخيمة، عجمان..

الموانئ الرئيسية: أبو ظبي، دبيّ، خور فكّان، الشارقة، أمّ القيوين.....

المنتجات المعدنية\الأولية: .البترول (٢،٦ م. برميل\يوم)، الغاز.....
المنتجات الصناعية: .البتروكيميائيات، موادّ البناء............
المنتجات الزراعية: .السمك، التمر، الخضر، البيض، اللبن، اللؤلؤ......
قطاع الخدمات: .السياحة، المصارف.....................

Ex. 7 1 تكاليف التشغيل 3 على الأكثر 2 عقود قصيرة الأجل 1
4 أطفال ضعفاء الجسم 6 تدريب عملي 5 الخرج السنوي
Ex. 8 1 الصواريخ طويلة المجال 2 بلاد دائم العضوية
3 لأساتذة واسعون العلم 4 دولة ضعيفة الاقتصاد
5 تجارب ممتازة النتائج 6 مع المرشّح المناسبين الأهلية
Ex. 9 1 ... ولا نعرف عنوانهم الجديد؟ 2 ... ولا تكفينا أبداً.
3 ... ونحن سنشكرهم وسنجاوب جوابًا إيجابيًا.
4 ... والحكومة ترفض مثل هذا التطوّر.
5 ... وهو يعرف جدول الأعمال تمامًا.
Ex. 10 (possible answers:) 1 توجد أعلى سلطة عند المرشد وهو معيّن مودى الحياة.
2 مجلس صيانة الدستور يراجع مرشحّين الانتخابات ويراجع القوانين المقترحة. ودور البرلمان هو اقتراح قوانين جديدة.

Chapter 15.

Ex. 1 (possible answer:)

من: قسم الأمن	إلى: جميع الأقسام؛ الألواح
التاريخ: ٢٧\٦\٦.	الإشارة: أمن ٣٦٨

الموضوع: إعادة استعمال المدخل الشمالي

يشير قسم الأمن إلى مذكّرته رقم ٣٦٥ من ٢٥\٥\٦. ويؤكّد أن المدخل الشمالي (جنب قسم الهندسة) سيعود مفتوحًا ابتداءً من الساعة السابعة في يوم السبت أوّل تموز.

مدير قسم الأمن

Ex. 2 (possible answer:)

ص. ب. ٦٤٧٤
أبو ظبي ١٢\١٠\٠٦
الإشارة: بوليصة رقم ١٢٢٤
قسم التعويض
شركة "الوطن" للتأمين
تحية طيّبة وبعد
أرفق بهذا نسخة نموذج طلب تعويض أرسلته لكم في الشهر الماضي بخصوص الخسارة الناتجة من حادث في تاريخ ١١\٩\٠٦ . وحتّى اليوم لم استلم جوابًا عليه.
أرجو أن تتفضّلوا بجواب الطلب المذكور في أقرب وقت الممكن.
وتفضّلوا بقبول فائق الاحترام
المخلص
....

Ex. 3 5, 7, 9, 2, 8, 4, 10, 6, 1, 3

Ex. 4 The upper line is from a typewriter; you have to shift to get the final and/or isolated letter forms. The lower line is from a computer, in which the program configurates letter forms automatically, the shift being used only for alternative letters or symbols.

Ex. 5 (possible answer:)

القاهرة في ٣٠\٩\٠٦
أخي العزيز
تحية طيّبة وبعد
أرسل لك بهذه الرسالة كم صورةً اشتريتها أمس وأنا ذهبت لزيارة الأهرام في جيزة. لا يمكننا الاعتقاد كيف بنوها قبل ألوف من السنوات بدون أيّة آلات حديثة.
غداً نعمل رحلةً على النيل تنظّمها وكالة سفر محلّية.
سلّم على كلّ العائلة من طرفي وأراكم بعد قليل،
المخلص
....

Ex. 6 (possible answer:)

تونس في ٨\٧\٠٦

أخي العزيز
تحية طيّبة وبعد
من طرف جميع الأصدقاء أشكرك على رسالتك اللطيفة. وجدنا بالفعل كتاب التعليمات وهو مرفق بهذا الخطاب.
يسرّني أنّ شغلك يجري جيّداً. كانت حفلة الأستاذ عظيمةً ومن الواضح أنّ الكتب تسرّه كثيراً. ألقى خطابًا جميلاً.
إن شاء الله يساعدك الكتاب وتعمل صوراً جميلةً هناك.
و يسلّم عليك كلّ الصفّ
المخلص
....

† (آلة للتصوير الرقمي digital ['numerical'] camera)

Chapter 16.

Ex. 1 1 خمسة وثلاثون طنًّا *khamsa wa-{thalāthūn} ṭunnan*
2 خمسة عشر واطًا *khamsat 'ashar wāṭan*
3 بأربعة دواليب *bi-'arba'a dawālīb*
4 البراميل الخمسئة\الخمس مئة *al-barāmīl al-khams {mi'a}*
5 مركّب بواسطة ستّة براغي *murakkab bi-wāsiṭat sitta barāghī*
6 شحن آلفي طنّ *shaḥn 'ālfay ṭunn*
7 أقلّ من الأطنان الخمسة المطلوبة *'aqall min al-'aṭnān al-khamsa l-maṭlūba*
8 سلك حامل أثني عشر ولتًا *silk ḥāmil {ithnay 'ashar} voltan*
9 ثمانية لترات بنزين وعشرون من الديزل *thamāniya litrāt binzīn wa-{'ishrūn} min ad-dīzil*
10 يكلّف ثلاثة وثلاثين ريالاً *yukallif thalātha wa-thalāthīn riyālan.*

Ex. 2 1 ستّة محركات جديدة 2 دفع مئتي دينار
3 في أربعة دواليب 4 الطلمبات القوية الثلاثة

5 الأشهر الاثنا عشر 6 الصواميل البلاستيكية الأربعة وعشرون
7 خلال الساعات الأربعة وعشرين
8 في الصهريج ذي اللترات الثلاثمئة\الثلاث مئة

Ex. 3

- †سير ≈ *sīr* or *sayr*, verbal noun, related to سيّارة already known, سير = 'drive, journey'. (NB: pronunciation is *sayr*.)
- †توقّف ≈ *tawaqquf*, Form V verbal noun; we know root وقف, توقّف 'stopping'.
- † تقلّ ≈ *taqall, taqull* or *taqill*, Form I doubled verb related to قليل already known. تقلّ عن ≈ 'is less/fewer than'. (Second principal part is in fact *yaqillu*).
- † أخرج ≈ *'akhrij*, † أدخل ≈ *'adkhil*, Form IV imperatives, roots خرج and دخل respectively. أخرج ≈ 'take out', أدخل ≈ 'insert'. (NB: These are not the Form I imperatives اخرج *ukhruj* and ادخل *udkhul* 'go out/in', which begin with a *weak vowel*; see B 1 and B 25.)
- †قياس ≈ *qiyās*; we know قاس يقيس *qāsa yaqīsu* I 'to measure'. قياس ≈ 'measure(ment)'; عصا قياس ≈ 'gauge, dipstick'.
- †...امسح ≈ *imsaḥ-*, imperative of Form I verb مسح which we know as 'to scan'. From this and the context, امسحها *imsaḥha* ≈ 'wipe it'.
- †شابه ≈ *shābih*, Form I active participle. We know شبه 'resemblance'. شابه ≈ 'resembling it, similar to it'.
- † أدخل ≈ *'adkhil*, see أخرج above.

(possible answer:) يجب أن المحرّك يكون على درجة حرارة التشغيل (مثلاً بعد سير ١٠ كم دون توقّف). يجب أيضاً أن تقف على سطح أفقي. أجرخ عصا القياس من المحرّك ونظّفه بمنديل ورقي مثلاً. ثمّ أدخله مرّة ثانية في أنبوبه حتّى النهاية وأخرجه وانظره. يجب أن يكون مستوى الزيت بين العلامتين على العصا. والمهمّ ألاّ يزيد مستوى الزيت عن العلامة الأعليا.

* The preposition حوالي is seen here as an adverb, 'approximately', with لتراً واحداً in the accusative as the direct object of تبلغ .

Chapter 17.

Ex. 1 1 *khamsa u-'ishrīn bi-l-mīya* 2 *thalāthat 'akhmās*
3 *'arba'a wa-'iḥd'ashar 'ala/min ithn'ashar*
4 *thamāniyat 'amtār bi-th-thāniya* 5 *tis'a 'ala/min 'ishrīn*
6 *sitta wa-khamsat 'asbā'*
7 *khamsa kīlo(ghrāmāt) bi-l-mitr al-murabba'*
8 *thalātha u-thalāthīn faṣla/nuqṭa thalātha* 9 *fī thulthay al-'amthāl*
10 *ḥarārat mitay daraja mi'awīya*
11 *tis'a 'ala thalātha yusāwī thalātha*
12 *mīya nāqiṣ ithnayn u-sab'īn yusāwī thamāniya u-'ishrīn*

Ex. 2 1 ١٠٠ كم\ساعة *mīt {mi'at} kilumitr bi s-sā'a*
2 ٧ = ٩ : ٦٣ *thalātha u-sittīn {wa-sittūn} 'ala/min tis'a yusāwī sab'a.* 3 بين ٣٤ و٣٦°م *bayn 'arba'a u-thalāthīn {'arba' wa-thalāthīn} wa-sitta u-thalāthīn {sitt wa-thalāthīn} daraja mi'awīya*
4 ٪٢٦ = ٢٠٠ : ٥٢ *ithnayn u-khamsīn {ithnān wa-khamsūn} 'ala/min mitayn {mi'atayn} yusāwī sitta u-'ishrīn bi-l-mīya {wa-'ishrīn bi-l-mi'a}* 5 ٣ × ٢٧ *sab'a u-'ishrīn {wa-'ishrūn} fī thalātha*
6 ٣ : ٢٧ *sab'a u-'ishrīn {wa-'ishrūn} 'ala/min thalātha*

Ex. 3 1 ٤٢ 2 ٣ = ب 3 ٣٢م٢ 4 ٤= ح 5 ٣،٦ = د 6 ٣٦ = أ
7 ٥- 8 ٣/٨

Ex. 4 1 سبب 2 مسوّدة 3 ممّا يلي 4 الحقّ 5 قال 5 كذب
6 المدّعى عليه 7 عليّ 8 الحقّ 8 أرسل 9 سالم 10 نظافة 11 حارّ\سخن
12 ضرب

Ex. 5 1 أرسل لنا لو سمحت المستند الإحصائي.
2 أرسل لنا لو سمحت المستند الشامل.
3 أرسل لنا لو سمحت الوثيقة الشاملة.
4 انظر لو سمحت الوثيقة الشاملة.
5 انظر لو سمحت المحتويات الشاملة.
6 انظر لو سمحت المحتويات التمهيدية.
7 تستنتج المسوّدة استنتاجًا إيجابيًا.

8. تستنتخ نصّه استنتاجًا إيجابيًا.
9. يقترح نصّه استنتاجًا إيجابيًا.
10. تقترح المعطيات استنتاجًا إيجابيًا.
11. تقترح المعطيات استنتاجًا معقّداً.
12. تثبت المعطيات استنتاجًا معقّداً.
13. تثبت الجداول استنتاجًا معقّداً.
14. تثبت الجداول استنتاجًا واضحًا.

Ex. 6 (possible answer:) يعرض الجدول أرقام مئوية لوضع الفقر في ثمانية بلدان عربية خلال أواخر القرن العشرين. ومن الواضح أنّ الفقر انخفض في عدّة بلدان في الشرق الأوسط ولكنّه ارتفع في أفريقيا الشمالية الغربية كما ننظر من أرقام موريتانيا والجزائر وتونس والمغرب. إنّ أكبر فرق بين البلدان الممثّلة هنا يوجد في جيبوتي أي زيادة الفقر بالنسبة أعلى من ٣٠٪ في مدّة ٦ سنوات. أفضل حالة هي مصر بانخفاض ٣٠٪ تقريبًا بين ١٩٩٥ و١٩٩٩. أرقام الجزائر قابلة للاهتمام: البلاد الوحيد المنتجة للنفط وعندها ارتفاع نسبي يساوي ٦٥٪ في ٧ سنوات (من ١٤٪ في ١٩٨٨ إلى ٢٤٪ في ١٩٩٥). ولا ننس خطّ الفقر المطبّق في الأمم المتّحدة وهو دخل دولار واحد باليوم.

Chapter 18.

Ex. 1 (possible answers:) 1 من يحكم الدعوى في محكمة
2 نصّ تمهيدي 3 إعادة كتابة نصّ بلغة ثانية
4 غير مريض 5 من على رأس سفارة نيابةً عن سفير
6 عمل صورةً 8 نظام تتبقه سلطة البلاد 7 قانون أساسي لبلاد
9 غير 12 اتّفاقية مكتوبة 11 فكّر نفس الشيء 10 جزء
13 تحرير نصوص على الكمبوتر 14 إنتاج كسور النفط المختلفة
15 الأرض بين جبلين 16 اتّفاقية لدفع تعويض في حالة كارثة
17 جملة تبتدئ بفعلها 18 من يمثّل جماعة ويتكلّم نيابةً عنها
19 كممثّل شخص ما
20 البلدان على الساحل الغربي للمحيط الهادي
21 مدة مئة سنة 22 لم يستقبل أو يستلم
23 الوضع الّذي يحدث شيئ فيه

24 كيف يعمل شخص بعد فعل أو قول شخص آخر
Ex. 2 (possible answers:) 1 ... فأتكلّم مع مساعده\مساعدته.
2 ... فليسألوا. 4 سنؤيّده ... 3 ... لكان هذا استثماراً ممتازاً.
5 ترجم لي هذا النصّ ... 6 ... فسنطلبه من مجلس الإدارة.
7 ... لكنّا نريد استشار الوزير. 8 ... فليرسل نائباً.
9 ... فإنّ ب يساوي ١٢. 10 ... فأطلب أن يقدّم شكوةً مكتوبةً.
Ex. 3 1 استهلك 2 جاوب 3 تقريباً 4 نهائي 5 دخل 6 تمّ
7 طقّس ناشف 8 جنوب 9 بريء 10 على الأقلّ 11 مستفيد العون
12 عدوّ 13 آخر 14 بسبب 15 يساراً 16 معتدل 17 مؤقّت 18 جزئي
Ex. 4 (possible answers:) 1 دراسةً طويلةً 2 بناءً 3 نظراً ل 4 طالبين
5 ردّاً على 6 جراحًا 7 منتظرين 8 وقتاً، شرحًا 9 احتجاجًا
10 زملاء، مشرفين
Ex. 5 (possible answers:) (a)

عاجل

من: قسم الإنتاج — إلى: الألواح

التاريخ: ٧\١\١٨. — الإشارة: إنتاج ٣٥٥

الموضوع: المشغل رقم ٣

بسبب حريق حدث في ٧\١\١٢. في القطاع الكهربي سيظلّ المشغل رقم ٣ مسكّراً لمدّة غير محدودة.
سيُستخدم في محلاّت أخرى (انظر ملحق هذا الإعلان) الموظّفون المستخدمون عادةً في المشغل رقم ٣ وهذا حتّى أعلان آخر.

نائب مدير قسم الإنتاج

نسخ: أقسام شؤون الموظّفين والأمن
مشرفي المشاغل ١ و٢ و٣.

(b)

عاجل

من: قسم الإنتاج　　　إلى: الألواح

التاريخ: ٢٩\١١\٠٧.　　　الإشارة: إنتاج ٣٥٧

الموضوع: المشغل رقم ٣

يشار إلى إعلان رقم ٣٥٥ من قسم الإنتاج بتاريخ ٨\١\٠٧.

ويعلن أنّ المشغل رقم ٣ سيعود مفتوحاً ابتداءً من

الساعة الثامنة في يوم السبت ٣\٢\٠٧.

ويجب علي جميع الموظّفين المستخدمين عادةً في المشغل المذكور

أن يستأنفوا وظائفهم هناك من ذلك الوقت.

وتشكر الإدارة جميع الموظّفين على تعاونهم خلال هذه المدّة.

نائب مدير قسم الإنتاج

نسخ: أقسام شؤون الموظّفين والأمن

مشرفي المشاغل ١ و٢ و٣.

Ex. 6　1 تمّ استبدال البرنامج مؤقّتًا تمهيداً لتوسيع القسم.
2 من الممكن أن تجري دراسة المعطيات مدّةً طويلةً.
3 تمّ حلّ مشكلة البرمجة بمساعدة خبير من المكتب المركزي.
4 تمّ استلام ثاني شحن أمس. 5 قاموا باستلام ثاني شحن أمس.

Ex. 7

أولاً – مبادئ الإدارة المنتجة

١ بناء الإدارة

٢ الربح والخسارة

٣ الاستثمارات

أ الاستثمار الرأسمالي

ب استثمارات طويلة الأجل

ج استثمارات قصيرة ومتوسّطة الأجل

٤ تمويل تكاليف التشغيل

(possible further headings:)

٥ الاستخدام

أ التخطيط

ب الإدارة
٦ التأمين
ثانيًا - الإنجاز العملي

Ex. **8** (possible answers:) 1 وهو محاسب
2 نشكّ في ضبطها 3 يتظاهرون ضدّ الزيارة الرسمية
4 طالبًا تأييدنا. 6 نحن استغربنا منه. 5 ولم نعرف الظروف؟
7 طالبًا إرسالها الفوري. 8 هي مؤسّسة على معطيات جديدة.
9 وأنت نسيت أهمّ نقطة. 10 شاكرةً جميع الحاضرين.
Ex. **9** 1 الخبر ممتاز - دفع أرباح نقدية بنسبة ٥٠٪.
2 يشكرهم على ثقتهم واعتمادهم.
3 الربح فوق العادي.
4 يشكرهم لجهودهم في وضع أسس نجاحات البنك.
5 إنّ الربح مؤسس علي القيمة الاسمية للأسهم.
6 مجلس الإدارة يقرّر سياسة البنك العامة والجهاز التنفيذي ينجز ويحقّق هذه السياسة.
7 في اللغة المصرفية "منتج" يساوي نوع الاستثمار.
8 إشارة طيّبة إلى قوة اقتصاد الكويت هي الفائدة على الأسهم، وأيضًا الـ"نجاحات المتتالية" المذكورة.
Ex. **10** 1 النسبة الفلسطينية أعلى من الإسرائيلية فيما يتعلّق بطلبة التعليم دون الدرجة الجامعية الأولى (عمود ٢) ولكنّها أوطأ بكثير فيما يتعلّق بالتعليم الجامعي (العمودان ٣ و٤). وهذا من المتوقّع نظراً للوضع الاجتماعي في فلسطين.
2 الأرقام الكويتية عادية في العمودين ٢ و٤ ولكنّها على مستوى صفر بالنسبة إلى الدرجة الجامعية الأولى - كيف؟
3 في جيبوتي (٦٨،٩٥٪).
4 انظر البحرين ومصر. نسباتهما قريبان ولكنهما يختلفان كثيراً في الاقتصاد (عدد السكّان، مستوى المعيشة، موادّ أوّلية).

Vocabulary index

Numbers indicate the chapter (or chapter/paragraph) containing the first or most useful appearance of the word. Words always preceded by the article ..الـ *al-* (etc.) are listed with the article, but in their own alphabetical position. For brevity, the particle 'to' is omitted from the English infinitive. The sign → refers a broken plural to its singular, wherever the two entries are not adjacent.

differ (from) 17
أخرج *'akhraja* IV take out 16
خطر ← أخطار
خطاب ← أخطبة
أخلص *'akhlaṣa* IV
be sincere, loyal 15
خمس ← أخماس
إخوان *'ikhwān* brethren 3
أخ ← إخوة
أدار *'adāra* IV manage 4
أدان *'adāna* IV convict 7
أدخل *'adkhala* IV insert 16
دليل ← أدلّة
دور ← أدوار
دواء ← أدوية
دين ← أديان
أرملة, أرمل ← أرامل
ربح ← أرباح
ربع ← أرباع
ارتكم *irtákama* VIII perpetrate 7
أرزّ *'aruzz* rice 5
أرفق (ب) *'arfaqa* IV *(bi-)*
enclose (with) 15
أرمل\أرملة أرامل *'armal(a)*
'arāmil widower, widow 3
زمن ← أزمان
زوج ← أزواج
أسطوانة ← أساطين
سبع ← أسباع
أستاذ *'ustādh* (also:) see 10/5
استجابة *istijāba*
positive response 12

استحال *istaḥāla* X
be unthinkable 11
استخدم *istakhdama* X
recruit, engage 2
استشفى *istashfa* X
seek a cure 2
استغرق *istaghraqa* X last 4
استغلّ *istaghalla* X exploit 7
استقال *istaqāla* X resign 2
استمارة *istimāra*
form (document) 9
استنتج *istantaja* X conclude
(draw a conclusion) 17
استوصف *istawṣafa* X
consult (a doctor) 2
سدس ← أسداس
سرّ ← أسرار
أساس ← أسس
أسّس *'assasa* II establish 12
أسطوانة أساطين *'usṭuwāna*
'asāṭīn disk 15
سلك ← أسلاك
سنّ ← أسنان
إسهام ب *'is-hām bi-* making
(someone) share in 12
سهم ← أسهم
شبه ← أشباه
اشتغل *ishtághala* VIII work 2
شراب ← أشربة
صاحب ← أصحاب
أصدر *'aṣdara* IV
issue, declare, pronounce 7

أصلح *'aṣlaḥa* IV reform 11
ضرر ← أضرار
أطفأ *'aṭfa'a* IV switch off 15
أطلسي see محيط
أطلق *'aṭlaqa* IV fire 13
أطلنطي see محيط
أعاد *'a'āda* IV + vb. noun (do) again, see 12
إعادة *'i'āda:* إعادة الإنشاء *'i'ādat al-'inshā'* restructuring, إعادة البناء *'i'ādat al-binā'* reconstruction, إعادة التوزيع *'i'ādat at-tawzī'* redistribution, إعادة الحساب *'i'ādat al-ḥisāb* recalculation 12
أعان (في) *'a'āna* IV *(fī* thing*)* subsidise 3
اعترف (ب) *i'taráfa* VIII *(bi-)* confess, admit (to) 15
اعتماد (إلى) *i'timād ('ila)* accreditation (to) 10; see أوراق
اعتمد على *i'támada* VIII *'ala* rely on 4
عدوّ ← أعداء
عرس ← أعراس
عزيز ← أعزاء
عشر ← أعشار
عشاء ← أعشية
إعلام see وسائل
غداء ← أغدية
غذاء ← أغذية
غلط ← أغلاط
أفقي *'ufuqī* horizontal 16
اقترض (من) *iqtárada* VIII *(min)* borrow (from) 12
اقتضى *iqtáḍa* VIII necessitate 10
إقرار *'iqrār* confirmation 14
أقرض *'aqraḍa* IV lend to 12
قسط ← أقساط
أقصى see شرق
أقلّ: على الأقلّ *'ala l-'aqall* at least 12
قمر ← أقمار
اكتسى ب *iktása* VIII *bi-* be clothed with/in 13
كذب ← أكذاب
كرد ← أكراد
إكرام *'ikrām* deference, إكرامًا ل *'ikrāman li-* in honour of 9
إكرامي *'ikrāmī* courtesy (adj.) 10
التزم *iltázama* VIII be obliged 10
ألغى *'algha* IV cancel, abolish 11
اللتان *'allatān* who, which 5
اللذان *'alladhān* who, which 5
الله: see بسم , حمد
اللواتي *'allawātī* who, which 5
آلة تصوير *'ālat taṣwīr* camera 15
آلة مسح *'ālat masḥ* scanner 15
لوحة ← ألواح
أمام: إلى الأمام *'ila l-'amām* forwards, أمامي *'amāmī* forward (adjective) 16
امتياز *imtiyāz* (also:) concession 10

أمير ← أمراء

أمر: لأمر ما *li-'amrin mā*
for some reason 11

مرض ← أمراض

إمرأة (المرأة) نسوان *'imra'a (al-mar'a) niswān* woman 3

مطر ← أمطار

ملح ← أملاح

ملك ← أملاك

أمّم *'ammama* II nationalise 4; *'umam* see برنامج

أموال *'amwāl* (pl., also:) funds, resources 4

أمير أمراء *'amīr 'umarā'* prince, emir 11

أنبوب أنابيب *'unbūb 'anābīb* pipe, tube 16

أنتما *'antuma* you both 5

أنتنّ *'antunna* you (f. pl.) 5

ناد\النادي ← أندية

إنساني *'insānī* human(e) 4

نسيج ← أنسجة

إنشاء see إعادة

نصف ← أنصاف

نظر ← أنظار

نظام ← أنظمة

انعقد *in'áqada* be convened 4

انفرادي *infirādī* unilateral 10

انفصل (عن) *infáṣala* VII *('an)* separate, secede (from) 11

انقلب *inqálaba* VIII be overthrown 2

إنمائي see برنامج

أنهى *'anha* IV bring to an end 5

هدف ← أهداف

هرم ← أهرام

أهلية *'ahlīya* qualification 2; see حرب

وجع ← أوجاع

أوراق الاعتماد *'awrāq al-i'timād* credentials 10

أوصى ب *'awṣa* IV *bi-* recommend 18

أولّي *'awwalī* primary, basic 12

إيّا... *'iyyā-* see 9/6

أيّتها see أيّها

إيران *'īrān* Iran 11

أيّها\أيّتها *'ayyuha/'ayyatuha* vocative particle, see 10/6

ب

بارد *bārid* cold 5

باق\الباقي *bāqin, al-bāqī* (weak) remainder (of subtraction) 17

بحيرة ← بحائر

البحر الأبيض (المتوسّط) *al-baḥr al-'abyaḍ (al-mutawassiṭ)* Mediterranean Sea, البحر الأحمر *al-baḥr al-'aḥmar* Red Sea 13

بحيرة بحائر *buḥayra baḥā'ir* lake 13

بدّ: لا بدّ من (أنّ) *lā budda min* + verbal noun/*'anna* there is no escaping/avoiding 11

بدل أبدال *badal 'abdāl*

benefit, allowance 2
برّاد *barrād* metalworker 2
برادة *birāda* metalwork 2
برّادة *barrāda* refrigerator 5
برغي ← براغي
برامج *barāmij* (pl., also:) software 15
برد *bard* cold(ness) 13
برغي براغي *burghī barāghī* screw 16
برمجة *barmaja* programming 15
برنامج الأمم المتّحدة الإنمائي *barnāmaj al-'umam al-muttáḥida l-'inmā'ī* United Nations Development Program, UNDP 12
برهان براهين *burhān barāhīn* proof 7
برهن على *barhana* IQ *'ala* prove 7
بريء أبرياء (من) *barī' 'abriyā' (min)* innocent (of) 7
صندوق ← بريدي
بسم الله الرحمن الرحيم *bi-sm illāh ar-raḥmān ar-raḥīm* in the name of God, the Merciful, the Compassionate 10
بطّارية *baṭṭārīya* battery 16
بعد see تحية
بعد يبعد (عن) *ba'uda yab'udu* I *('an)* be distant (from) 13
بل *bal* but rather 11
بلد ← بلاد
بلاستيك *blāstīk* plastic 16
بلد بلاد *balad bilād* (also:) country 18
بلدية *baladīya* (also:) town council 3; see رئيس
بناء أبنية *binā' 'ábniya* construction, بناءً على *binā'an 'ala* on the basis of 9; see إعادة
بنّاء *bannā'* builder 2
بند بنود *band bunūd* clause, article, paragraph 9
بنية تحتية *binya taḥtīya* infrastructure 12
بوليصة ← بواليص
بوزة *būza* ice, ice cream 5
بوليصة بواليص *būlīṣa bawālīṣ* policy 9
بيانات *bayānāt* (pl., also:) details, particulars 9
بياني *bayānī* graphical 15
بيئة *bī'a* environment 17
بيرة *bīra* beer 5
بيطاري *baiṭārī* veterinary 6

ت

تأسّس *ta'assasa* V be established, founded 12
تالٍ\التالي *tālin, at-tālī* (weak) (the) following 17
تأمرك *ta'amraka* IIQ be(come) Americanised 7
تاييداً ل *ta'yīdan li-* in support of 9

تبريد *tabrīd* refrigeration 2
تثلّج *tathallaja* V
become frozen 13
تجسيد *tajsīd* embodiment 12
تجمّع *tajamma'a* V
be accumulated 13
تحتية see بنية
تحرير see منظّمة
تحية *taḥīya* greeting,
تحية طيّبة وبعد *táḥiya ṭayyiba wa-ba'du* see 15
تدحرج *tadaḥraja* IIQ roll (itself) 7
تدريب أثناء العمل *tadrīb 'athnā' al-'amal* on-the-job training 12
ترجم يترجم *tarjama yutarjimu* IQ
translate 7
ترس تروس *tirs turūs*
gear(wheel) 16
ترسيخ *tarsīkh* securing 12
ترشّح *tarashshaḥa* V
catch a cold 6
تركّز (في) *tarakkaza* V *(fī)*
concentrate (on) 5
تركيا *túrkiya* Turkey 11
ترس → تروس
تزلزل *tazalzala* IIQ
quake (esp. of the earth) 7
تزوّج (من\ب\على) *tazawwaja* V
(min/bi-/'ala) get married (to) 3
تساقط *tasāquṭ* fall
(e.g. of snow) 13
تسع أتساع *tus' 'atsā'* a ninth 17

تسلسل *tasalsala* IIQ form a chain or sequence; *tasalsul* sequence, succession 7
تشجيع (على) *tashjī' ('ala)* incentive, encouragement (to) 4
تشريفات *tashrīfāt* (pl.) protocol 10
تصادف *taṣādafa* VI happen by chance; *taṣāduf* coincidence 9
تصادم (ب\مع) *taṣādama* VI *(bi-, ma')* collide (with); *taṣādum* collision 9
تصنيف *taṣnīf* classification 18
تصوير see آلة
تضامن *taḍāmun* solidarity 12
تعالج *ta'ālaja* VI
undergo treatment 6
تعطيل *ta'ṭīl* suspension 14
تعريف ب *ta'rīf bi-*
definition of 12
تعهّد *ta'ahhada* V
commit oneself 10
تقاعد *taqā'ada* VI retire,
تقاعد *taqā'ud* retirement 2;
see معاش
تقدير *taqdīr* estimate 5
تقرير: تقرير شفوي *taqrīr shafawī*
note verbale 10; see رفع
تكييف *takyīf* airconditioning 2
تلفز *talfaza* IQ televise 7
تلفزة *talfaza* television 7
تلفن *talfana* IQ telephone 7
تم يتم *tamma yatimmu* I

(come to an) end, see 10/3
تمتّع ب *tamatta'a* V *bi-* enjoy 12
تمرير *tamrīr* passing 14
تمهيد *tamhīd* preparation, تمهيداً ل *tamhīdan li-* preparatory to 9; تمهيدي *tamhīdī* provisional, preparatory 17
تنازل عن (ل) *tanāzala* VI *'an* (thing) waive; *(li-)* (person) renounce (in favour of); *tanāzul ('an)* waiver (of) 9
تناول *tanāwala* III take (food, drink) 5
تهنئة تهانئ *tahni'a tahāni'* congratulation 15
توجّب *tawajjaba* V be necessary 18
توجّه إلى *tawajjaha* V *'ila* turn towards 10
توزيع see إعادة
توشوش *tawashwasha* IIQ whisper 7
توفّر *tawaffara* V abound 11
توفير *tawfīr* provision 12
توفيق *tawfīq* Tawfiq 3
توقّف *tawaqquf* stopping 16

ث

ثقة *thiqa* confidence, trust 18
ثلث أثلاث *thulth 'athlāth* a third 17
ثلج ثلوج *thalj thulūj* snow, تثلج السماء *tathluj as-samā'* it is snowing 13
ثمّ *thumma* and then 11
ثمن أثمان *thumn 'athmān* an eighth 17
ثنائي *thunā'ī* bilateral 10
ثورة *thawra* revolution 11

ج

جبر: (علم) الجبر *('ilm) al-jabr* algebra 17
جبنة *jubna* cheese 5
جدول جداول *jadwal jadāwil* (also:) table, chart 17; جدول أعمال *jadwal 'a'māl* agenda 4
جراء: من جراء *min jarā'* on account of 7
جرّاح *jarrāḥ* surgeon 2
جرثوم ← جراثيم
جراحة *jirāḥa* surgery 2
جرح *jaraḥa yajraḥu* I injure 6
جرثوم\جرثومة جراثيم *jurthūm(a) jarāthīm* germ, microbe 6
جرم أجرام *jurm 'ajrām* offence 7
جرى يجري *jara yajrī* I flow, see 10/4
جزيل ← جزال
جزر: جزر القمر *juzur al-qamar* Comores 18; ← جزيرة
جزيرة جزر *jazīra juzur* island
جزيل جزال *jazīl jizāl* abundant 18
جسم أجسام *jism 'ajsām* body 6
جسوس جواسيس *jasūs jawāsīs* spy, جسوسية *jasūsīya*

espionage 10
جغرافية *jughrāfīya* geography 13
جماهيرية *jamāhīrīya* Jamahiriya ('State of the Masses') 4
جمع *jam'* addition 17
جملة جمل *jumla jumal* sentence 13
جمعية *jam'īya* association 3; meeting 18
جنائي *jinā'ī* criminal (case, law etc.) 7
جنسية *jinsīya* nationality 10
جهاز أجّهزة *jihāz 'ajhiza* appliance, apparatus, جهاز تدوير *jihāz tadwīr* drive, جهاز مسح *jihāz masḥ* scanner 15
جهد جهود *juhd juhūd* effort 4
جهة *jiha* side, direction, domain عن جهة واحدة *'an jiha wāḥida* unilaterally, عن جهتين *'an jihatayn* bilaterally 10; من جهة (أخرى) *min jihatin ('ukhra)* on the one (other) hand 11
جواز سفر *jawāz safar* passport 10
جسوس ← جواسيس
جوعان جوعى جياع *jaw'ān,* f. *jaw'a*, pl. *jiyā'* hungry 5

ح

حادث حوادث *ḥādith ḥawādith* accident 9
حارّ *ḥārr* hot 13
حاسب *ḥāsib* calculator 15
حاصل حواصل *ḥāṣil ḥawāṣil* product (of multiplication) 17
حال أحوال *ḥāl 'aḥwāl* expression of circumstance see 12/1-4
حالة *ḥāla* case, situation 10; حالة الطوارئ *ḥālat aṭ-ṭawāri'* state of emergency 12
حجم حجوم *ḥajm ḥujūm* volume 17
حدّ يحد *ḥadda yaḥuddu* I limit 4
حدوث *ḥudūth* occurrence 13
حديد *ḥadīd* iron 16
حذف يحذف *ḥadhafa yaḥdhifu* I delete 15
حرارة *ḥarāra* fever, temperature, heat 6
حريق ← حرائق
حرب أهلية *ḥarb 'ahlīya* civil war 10; حرب عالمية *ḥarb 'ālamīya* world war 11
حرّر *ḥarrara* II liberate, emancipate 11, edit 15
حريق حرائق *ḥarīq ḥarā'iq* fire 9
حساب *ḥisāb* calculation 17; see إعادة
حسّن *ḥassan* Hassan 15
حصانة *ḥaṣāna* immunity 10
حضرة *ḥaḍra* presence, see 10/5
حظي يحظى ب *ḥáẓiya yaḥẓa* I *bi-* enjoy 11
حفّار *ḥaffār* driller 2
حفلة *ḥafla* celebration, party 10

الحق عليه\معه *al-ḥaqq ʿalayhi/maʿahu* he is (in the) wrong/right 7

حقّق *ḥaqqaqa* II realise 11

حقن يحقن *ḥaqana yaqḥunu* I inject 6

حقنة حقن *ḥuqna ḥuqan* injection 6

حقوق *ḥuqūq* (also:) jurisprudence 7

حكم أحكام *ḥukm ʾaḥkām* judgment, rule 7; حكم ذاتي *ḥukm dhātī* autonomy 10

حكم يحكم على *ḥakama yaḥkumu* I *ʿala* judge, sentence 7

حلف *ḥilf* alliance 11

حليف ← حلفاء

حلو *ḥalw* sweet 5

حلويات *ḥalwayāt* sweets, dessert 5

حليف حلفاء *ḥalīf ḥulafāʾ* ally 11

الحمد لله *al-ḥamdu li-llah* ('praise (be) to God') thank heaven 15

حادث ← حوادث

حاصل ← حواصل

حوّل *ḥawwala* II transfer 4

حياد *ḥiyād* neutrality 11

خ

خبّاز *khabbāz* baker 2

خبازة *khibāza* bakery 2

خبر أخبار *khabar ʾakhbār* (also:) message 10

خبرة *khibra* experience 2

خبز أخباز *khubz ʾakhbāz* bread 5

خدمة *khidma* service 2; خدمات اجتماعية *khidmāt ijtimāʿīya* social services 3

خرج *kharj* expenditure 12

خرقة خرق *khirqa khiraq* rag 16

خزن يخزن\خزّن *khazana yakhzunu* I, *khazzana* II store 15

خسارة *khasāra* loss 4

خسر يخسر *khasira yakhsaru* I lose 4

خصوصًا *khuṣūṣan* (e)specially, particularly 13

خضع: بخضع ل *bi-khuḍuʿ li-* governed by 12

خطاب أخطبة *khiṭāb ʾakhṭiba* (also:) letter 15

خطر أخطار *khaṭar ʾakhṭār* danger, risk 9

خطّط *khaṭṭaṭa* II plan 2

خطّة خطط *khiṭṭa khiṭaṭ* plan, scheme 2

خضر *khuḍar* vegetables 5

خلط يخلط *khalaṭa yakhliṭu* I mix 5

خمر خمور *khamr khumūr* (m./f.) wine 5

خمس أخماس *khums ʾakhmās* a fifth 17

خوفًا على\من *khawfan ʿala* fearing for, *khawfan min* for fear of 9

خيّاط *khayyāṭ* tailor, خيّاطة *khayyāṭa* dressmaker 2

خياطة *khiyāṭa* sewing 2
خيمة see رأس

د

دافع دوافع *dāfi' dawāfi'* motivation 4
دائرة دوائر *dā'ira dawā'ir* directorate 4; circuit 16
دائم *dā'im* permanent 4
دجلة *dijla* Tigris 13
دحرج *daḥraja* IQ roll (something) 7
دحرجة *daḥraja* roll(ing) 7
دخل *dakhl* income 3
دخّن *dakhkhana* II smoke 6
درجة حرارة *darajat ḥarāra* temperature 6
دستور دساتير *dustūr dasātīr* constitution, statute 7
دعا يدعو إلى *da'a yad'ū* I *'ila* call for 11
دعوى ← دعاوى
دعم *da'm* support 12
دعوة *da'wa 'ila* call 11
دعوى دعاوى *da'wa da'āwa* case, lawsuit 7
دفتر دفاتر *daftar dafātir* register, ledger, notebook 17
دقيق دقاق *daqīq diqāq* fine 5
دلتا *dilta* delta 13
دليل أدلّة *dalīl 'adilla* directory 17
دم *dam* blood 6
دنيا *dunya* world 13
دواء أدوية *dawā' 'ádwiya* medicine, medication 6
دافع ← دوافع
دولاب ← دواليب
دائرة ← دوائر
دور أدوار *dawr 'adwār* rôle 4
دورة *dawra* round (of talks etc.) 4
دولاب دواليب *dūlāb dawālīb* wheel 16
دولي see صندوق
دوماً *dawman* constantly 11
دون *dūn* (also:) below 13
دوّن *dawwana* II place on record 10
ديزل *dīzil* diesel 16
دين أديان *dīn 'adyān* religion 11

ذ

ذاتي *dhātī* autonomous 11; see حكم
ذاكرة *dhākira* memory 15
ذكرى ذكريات *dhikra dhikrayāt* commemoration 10

ر

راجع *rāja'a* III review, revise 12
راديكالي *rādīkālī* radical 11
رأس الخيمة *ra's al-khayma* Ras al Khayma 13
رافق *rāfaqa* III accompany 10
ربح يربح *rabiḥa yarbaḥu* I profit 4
ربح أرباح *ribḥ 'arbāḥ* profit 4
ربط يربط (ب) *rabaṭa yarbuṭu* I *(bi-)* connect (with/to) 15

ربع أرباع *rub' 'arba'* a quarter 17
رتبة رتب *rutba rutab* grade, rank 2
رجل رجال *rajul rijāl* man 3
رجعي *raj'ī* reactionary 11
رحمن see بسم , عبد
رحلة see طيّران
رحيم see بسم
ردّ (ردود) فعل *radd* (pl. *rudūd) fi'l* reaction 11
رداً على *raddan 'ala* in reply to 15
ردود → ردّ
رخّص (ل ب) *rakhkhaṣa* II (*li-* person, *bi-* thing) license, permit 3
رخصة رخص *rukhṣa rukhaṣ* licence, permit 3
رسّخ *rassakha* II fix firmly 12
رسم رسوم *rasm rusūm* drawing, graph 15
رشح *rashḥ* a cold 6
رشيد *rashīd* Rashid 3
رطب *raṭb* humid 13
رطوبة *ruṭūba* humidity 13
رغبة رغبات (في) *raghba ragahabāt (fī)* wish (for), رغبةً في *raghbatan fī* aiming at, wishing for 9
رفض يرفض *rafaḍa yarfiḍu* I (also:) dismiss (a legal case) 7
رفع يرفع تقريراً إلى *rafa'a yarfa'u* I *taqrīran 'ila* report to 2
رقمي *raqmī* numerical, digital 15
روضة رياض (أطفال) *rawḍa riyāḍ ('aṭfāl)* kindergarten 3
ريح رياح *rīḥ riyāḥ* (f.) wind 13
رئيس بلدية *ra'īs baladīya* mayor 3

ز

زاد يزيد (إلى) *zāda yazīdu* I (*'ila)* add (to) 17
زائد *zā'id* plus 17
زبدة *zubda* butter 5
زجاج *zujāj* glass 16
زعيم زعماء *za'īm zu'amā'* leader 11
زلزال *zilzāl* shaking, rocking 7
زلزل *zalzala* IQ shake, rock 7
زمن أزمان *zaman 'azmān* time 11
زواج *ziwāj* marriage 3
زوج أزواج *zawj 'azwāj* husband 3
زوجة *zawja* wife 3
زوّر *zawwara* II falsify 7
زيادة *ziyāda* (also:) addition 17
زين *zayn* Zein 15

س

ساكن سكّان *sākin sukkān* inhabitant 3
سالم *sālim* healthy 6
ساوى *sāwa* III equal 17
سائد *sā'id* prevailing 10
سبّاك *sabbāk* plumber 2
سباكة *sibāka* plumbing 2
سبع أسباع *sub' 'asbā'* a seventh 17
سبق يسبق *sabaqa yasbiqu*

precede 17
سجّل *sajjala* II register 3
سحاب *saḥāb* clouds, سحابة سحب *saḥāba suḥub* cloud 13
سخن *sukhn* hot 5
سدّد *saddada* II repay 12
سدس أسداس *suds 'asdās* a sixth 17
سرّ يسرّ *sarra yasurru* I please, يسرّني ب *yasurrunī bi-* I am pleased by/at 15
سرّ أسرار *sirr 'asrār* secret (noun) 10
سرق يسرق *saraqa yasriqu* I steal 7
سرقة *sariqa* theft 7
سرّية *sirrīya* secrecy 5
سطح سطوح *saṭḥ suṭūḥ* surface 16
سعادة *sa'āda* Excellency, see 10/5
سفّر *saffara* II send (a person) 10
سفينة الفضاء *safīnat al-faḍā'* spaceship 13
سكّين → سكاكين
ساكن → سكّان
سكّر *sukkar* sugar 5
سكّر *sakkara* II shut 15
سكن *sakan* housing 3
سكّين سكاكين *sikkīn sakākīn* (m./f.) knife 5
سلسلة → سلاسل
سلاطة *salāṭa* salad 5
سلسل *salsala* IQ connect 7
سلسلة سلاسل *silsila salāsil* chain, series 7
سلك أسلاك *silk 'aslāk* wire 4
سلّم على *sallama* II *'ala* greet 15
سماء سماوات *samā' samāwāt* (m./f.) sky 13; see ثلج, مطر
سمسار → سماسير
سماء → سماوات
سمسار سماسير *simsār samāsīr* broker 9
سنّ أسنان *sinn 'asnān* tooth 6
سهم أسهم *sahm 'as-hum* share (of stock) 4
سوّاق *sawwāq* driver 2
سيادة *siyāda* Excellency, see 10/5
سير *sayr* journey 16
سيطر على *sayṭara* IQ *'ala* rule over 7
سيطرة *sayṭara* rule 7

ش

شاحنة *shāḥina* lorry, truck 12
شارك في *shāraka* III *(fī)* participate (in) 4
شامل *shāmil* comprehensive 9
شأن شؤون *sha'n shu'ūn* matter 11
شاهد شهود *shāhid shuhūd* witness 7
شبه أشباه: شبه *shibh 'ashbāh* resemblance, semi-, quasi-, see 4/4; شبه جزيرة أشباه جزر *shibh jazīra 'ashbāh juzur* peninsula, شبه قارّة *shibh qārra*

subcontinent 4
شحّم *shahhama* II lubricate 16
شحن يشحن *shahana yashhanu* I load, charge (a battery) 16
شحن *shahn* load 16
شخص ما *shakhsun mā* somebody or other 11
سراء *shirā'* purchase 5
شراب أشربة *sharāb 'ashriba* drink 5
شرط: ب\على شرط أنْ *bi-/'ala shart 'an* (+ subjunctive) on condition that, provided that 10
الشرق الأقصى *ash-sharq al-'aqsa* Far East 13
شريك ← شركاء
شريطةً *sharītatan* subject to 14
الشريعة *ash-sharī'a* Sharia (Muslim) law 7
شريك شركاء *sharīk shurakā'* partner, associate 4
شعب شعوب *sha'b shu'ūb* people 11
شغّل *shaghghala* II operate 4
شغل إضافي *shughl 'idāfī* overtime (work) 2
شفرة *shifra* cypher, code 10
شفوي see تقرير
شفوياً *shafawīyan* orally 17
شكراً *shukran* Thank you 9
شمس شموس *shams shumūs* (f.) sun 13; شمسي see صورة
شهادة *shahāda* (also:) testimony, evidence 7
شهد يشهد (ب\أنّ) *shahida yashhadu* I *(bi-, 'anna)* testify 7
شاهد ← شهود
شوربة *shōrba* soup 5
شوكة *shawka* fork 5
شؤون: شؤون الموظّفين *shu'ūn al-muwazzafīn* Personnel 2; ← شأن
شيخ شيوخ *shaykh shuyūkh* elder, senator 3
شيوعي *shuyū'ī* communist 11

ص

صاحب أصحاب *sāhib 'ashāb* holder, owner 9; صاحب عمل *sāhib 'amal* employer 4
صاروخ صواريخ *sārūkh sawārīkh* rocket 13
صامولة صواميل *sāmūla sawāmīl* nut (engineering) 16
صحيح ← صحاح
صحن صحون *sahn suhūn* plate 5
صحّة *sihha* (also:) correctness 10
صحيح صحاح *sahīh sihāh* true, correct 7
صداقة *sadāqa* friendship 12
صدر صدور *sadr sudūr* chest 6
صرّاف *sarrāf* moneychanger 2
صرّح ب *sarraha* II *bi-* assert 17
صغير صغار *saghīr sighār*

(also:) young 6

صفر *ṣifr* zero 13

صفة *ṣifa* capacity, function 9

صلاحية *ṣalāḥīya* competence 14

صلّح *ṣallaḥa* II repair 16

صلة *ṣila* connexion 10

صمام *ṣimām* valve, plug 16

صناعي see قمر

صندوق صناديق *ṣandūq ṣanādīq* fund 2; صندوق بريدي (ص.ب) *ṣandūq barīdī* post office box, POB 15; صندوق النقد الدولي *ṣandūq an-naqd ad-duwali* International Monetary Fund, IMF 12

صنّع *ṣanna'a* II industrialise 12

صهريج صهاريج *ṣahrīj ṣahārīj* tank (fuel etc.) 16

صهيوني *ṣahyūnī* Zionist 11

صاروخ ← صواريخ

صامولة ← صواميل

صوّت (ل\ضدّ) *ṣawwata* II *(li-, ḍidd)* vote (for/against) 11

صوّر *ṣawwara* II (also:) photocopy 15

صورة شمسية *ṣūra shamsīya* photograph 10

صيانة *ṣiyāna* preservation, guardianship 14

صيدلي صيادلة *ṣaidalī ṣayādila* pharmacist 6

صيدلية *ṣaidalīya* pharmacy 6

ض

ضابط ضبّاط *ḍābiṭ ḍubbāṭ* officer 4

ضخّ يضخّ *ḍakhkha yaḍukhkhu* I pump 16

ضخم ضخام *ḍakhm ḍikhām* vast 15

ضرّ يضرّ *ḍarra yaḍurru* I damage 7

ضرب *ḍarb* multiplication 17

ضرب يضرب (في) *ḍaraba yaḍribu* I *(fī)* multiply (by) 17

ضرر أضرار *ḍarar 'aḍrār* damage 7

ضغط ضغوط *ḍaghṭ ḍughūṭ* pressure 6

ضمان *ḍamān* guarantee 12; ضمان اجتماعي *ḍamān ijtimā'ī* social security 3

ضمن يضمن *ḍamina yaḍmanu* I guarantee 12

ط

طابع *ṭābi'* printer 15

طبّاخ *ṭabbākh* cook 2

طباخة *ṭibākha* cookery 2

طبخ يطبخ *ṭabakha yaṭbukhu* I cook 5

طبع *ṭab'* printing 15

طبيب أسنان *ṭabīb 'asnān* dentist 6

طبيعة *ṭabī'a* nature 13; طبيعي *ṭabī'ī* natural 9

طحين *ṭaḥīn* flour 5
طرابلس *ṭarābulus* Tripoli 4
طريقة ← طرائق
طرح *ṭarḥ* subtraction 17
طرح يطرح (من) *ṭaraḥa yaṭraḥu* I *(min)* subtract (from) 17
طرف ثالث *ṭaraf thālith* third party 9
طرئة طوارئ *ṭari'a ṭawari'* emergency 12
طريقة طرائق *ṭarīqa ṭarā'iq* way, manner 11
طرئة ← طوارئ ; see حالة, عون
طقس *ṭaqs* weather 13
طلبة *ṭaliba* demand 18
طوّر *ṭawwara* II develop 2
طيّب see تحية
طيران\رحلة في الفضاء *ṭayarān/ riḥla fi l-faḍā'* space flight 13

ظ

ظالم ظلاّم *ẓālim ẓullām* tyrant, oppressive 11
ظرف ظروف *ẓarf ẓurūf* circumstance 4
ظالم ← ظلاّم
ظلم يظلم *ẓalama yaẓlimu* I oppress 11
ظلم *ẓulm* oppression 11
ظهر ظهور *ẓahr ẓuhūr* back 6

ع

عاجز عجزة *'ājiz 'ajaza* disabled 6
عاجل *'ājil* urgent 15
عادي *'ādī* ordinary, غير عادي *ghayr 'ādī* extraordinary 4
عالج *'ālaja* III treat, cure 6; process 15
عالمي *'ālamī* (also:) universal 7; see حرب
عبد الرحمن *'abd ar-raḥmān* Abdulrahman 15
عبده *'abdo* Abdu 15
عجز *'ajz* disability 6
عاجز ← عجزة
عدّ يعدّ *'adda ya'uddu* I count, consider 12
عدل *'adl* just, fair 7
عدلية *'adlīya* justice 7
عدوّ أعداء *'adūw 'a'dā'* enemy 11
عديم *'adīm* lacking (in), un-, in-, see 4/2
عرس أعراس *'urs 'a'rās* wedding 3
عرض يعرض *'araḍa ya'riḍu* I display, show 15
عرض عروض *'arḍ 'urūḍ* display 15
عزل يعزل (عن) *'azala ya'zilu* I *('an)* dismiss (from) 2
عزل (عن) *'azl ('an)* dismissal (from) 2
عزيز أعزاء *'azīz 'a'izzā'* dear, beloved 10
عشاء أعشية *'ashā' 'áshiya*

dinner, supper 5
عشر أعشار *'ushr 'a'shār* a tenth 17
عصا عصي *'aṣa 'uṣī* stick; عصا قياس *'aṣa qiyās* gauge, dipstick 16
عصر عصور *'aṣr 'uṣūr* age, era, العصور\ القرون الوسطى *al-'uṣūr/al-qurūn al-wusṭa* the Middle Ages 11
عصا ← عصي
عصير *'aṣīr* juice 5
عضوية *'uḍwīya* membership 12
عطشان عطشى عطاش *'aṭshān,* f. *'aṭsha,* pl. *'iṭāsh* thirsty 5
عظيم عظماء *'aẓīm 'uẓamā'* huge; splendid 13
عفواً *'afwan* (I beg) Pardon 9
عقوبة *'uqūba* punishment 7
علاج *'ilāj* treatment 6
علامة *'alāma* signal, mark, sign 16
علاوة *'ilāwa* benefit, allowance 2
على علم ب *'ala 'ilm bi-* aware of 7; see جبر :علم
علني *'alanī* public 7
على *'ala* (also:) divided by, over 17
عملاً ب *'amalan bi-* in accordance with, pursuant to 9
عميل ← عملاء
عمود عواميد *'amūd 'awāmīd* column 17
عميل عملاء *'amīl 'umalā'* client 18
عناية *'ināya* care 16
عهد يعهد إلى ب *'ahida ya'hadu* I *'ila* (person) *bi-* (thing) entrust 12
عون *'awn* aid, عون الطوارئ *'awn aṭ-ṭawāri'* emergency aid 12
عيّن *'ayyana* II appoint 9

غ

غداء أغدية *ghadā' 'ághdiya* lunch 5
غذاء أغذية *ghidhā' 'ághdhiya* food 5
غطى يغطي *ghaṭa yaghṭī* I cover 13
غلط أغلاط *ghalaṭ 'aghlāṭ* error 15
غير: تأمين ضدّ الغير *ta'mīn ḍidd al-ghayr* third party insurance 9; see عادي

ف

فاض يفيض *fāḍa yafīḍu* I flood 9
فاكهة فواكه *fākiha fawākih* fruit 5
فائدة فوائد *fā'ida fawā'id* (monetary) interest 4
فائق *fā'iq* exceeding, highest 15
فتح يفتح *fataḥa yaftaḥu* I (also:) switch on 15
فترة فترات *fatra fatarāt* period 4
فحص فحوص *faḥṣ fuḥūṣ* examination, inquiry 2

فدائي *fidā'ī* guerrilla fighter 11
الفرات *al-furāt* Euphrates 13
فرع فروع *far' furū'* branch 9
فساد *fasād* corruption 5
فصل فصول *faṣl fuṣūl* chapter 17
فضاء *faḍā'* space, فضائي *faḍā'ī* space traveller, cosmonaut 13; see طيّران
فطور *faṭūr* breakfast 5
فعل see ردّ
فقر *faqr* poverty 17
فقير فقراء *faqīr fuqarā'* poor 3
فلسطين see منظّمة
فلسف *falsafa* IQ philosophise 7
فلسفة *falsafa* philosophy 7
فنجان فناجين *finjān fanājīn* cup 5
فهرس فهارس *fihris fahāris* index, catalogue, list 17
فاكهة → فواكه
فائدة → فوائد
فولاذ *fūlādh* steel 16
فولت\ڤولت *volt* volt 16
في *fī* (also:) times, multiplied by 17
فيزا\ڤيزا *vīza* visa 10
فيضان *fayaḍān* flood 9

ق

قابل ل *qābil li-* susceptible to, -able, -ible, see 4/2
قاتل قتّال *qātil quttāl* killer, murderer 7
قارّة *qārra* continent 4
قارن *qārana* III compare 5
قاس يقيس *qāsa yaqīsu* I measure 16
قام يقوم ب *qāma yaqūmu* I *bi-* undertake, see 10/2
قاوم *qāwama* III resist 11
قائم (قوّام) بالأعمال *qā'im* (pl. *quwwām*) *bi-l-'a'māl* chargé d'affaires 10
قائمة قوائم *qā'ima qawā'im* list, register 17
قاتل → قتّال
قتل *qatl* murder, homicide 7
قتل يقتل *qatala yaqtulu* I kill, murder 7
قد qad + *present tense* perhaps 5
قدّر *qaddara* II estimate 4
قذف *qadhf* libel, slander 7
قرينة → قرائن
قرن قرون *qarn qurūn* century 11; see عصر
قروي *qarawī* villager 13
قرينة قرائن *qarīna qarā'in* context 17
قسط أقساط *qisṭ 'aqsāṭ* (insurance) premium 9
قسم يقسم (على) *qasama yaqsimu* I *('ala)* divide (by) 17
قسمة *qisma* division (arith.) 17
قلّ يقلّ عن *qalla yaqillu* I *'an*

to be less/fewer than 16
قلب قلوب *qalb qulūb* heart 6
قليلاً ما *qalīlan mā* seldom 11
قمح قموح *qamaḥ qumūḥ* wheat 5
قمر أقمار *qamar 'aqmār* moon,
قمر صناعي *qamar ṣinā'ī*
satellite 13; see جزر
قمح ← قموح
قنصل قناصل *qunṣul qanāṣil*
consul, قنصلية *qunṣulīya*
consulate 10
قائم ← قوام
قائمة ← قوائم
قوة عاملة *quwa 'āmila*
workforce 2
قياس *qiyās* measurement 16;
see عصا
قيمة قيم *qīma qíyam* value 5

ك

كاذب *kādhib* false 17
كاراج *gārāj* garage 9
كارثة كوارث *kāritha kawārith*
disaster 9
كأس كؤوس *ka's ku'ūs* (f.)
a glass 5
كامل *kāmil* Kamil 15
كبير كبار *kabīr kibār* (also:)
old 6
كثيراً ما *kathīran mā* often 11
كذب يكذب *kadhaba yakdhibu* I
tell a lie 7
كذب أكذاب *kidhb 'akdhāb* lie 7
كريم ← كرام
كرد أكراد *kurd 'akrād* Kurd 11
كردستان *kurdistān* Kurdistan 11
كريم كرماء\كرام *karīm kuramā',*
kirām kind, generous 15, 18
كسر كسور *kasr kusūr* fraction 17
كفل يكفل *kafala yakfulu* I
sponsor, secure 10
كفيل كفلاء *kafīl kufalā'*
sponsor 10
كما *kama* as 11
كنّاس *kannās* sweeper 2
كارثة ← كوارث
كوكب كواكب *kawkab kawākib*
planet 13
كأس ← كؤوس

ل

لاإنساني *lā-'insānī* inhuman(e),
لاإنسانية *lā-'insānīya*
inhumanity 4
لاجئ *lāji'* refugee 10
لازم *lāzim* necessary 12
لاسلكي *lā-silkī* wireless 4
لامركزية *lā-markazīya*
decentralisation 4
لبن *laban* milk 5
لجوء *lujū'* asylum 10
لحام *liḥām* welding, butchery 2;
لحم ←
لحّام *laḥḥām* welder, butcher 2
لحم لحام *laḥm liḥām* meat 5
لصّ لصوص *liṣṣ luṣūṣ* thief 7

لقّح (ضدّ) *laqqaḥa* II *(ḍidd)* vaccinate (against) 6

لهجة *lahja* accent, tone (of speech) 11

لوحة ألواح *lawḥa 'alwāḥ* board 15

لوّن *lawwana* II colour 15

لون ألوان *lawn 'alwān* colour 15

ليل *layl* night(time) 13

م

ما *mā* + comparative how ...! 9; see أمر , شخص , قليل , كثير , يوم , نوع

ماء مياه *mā' miyāh* water 5; ماء الشرب\للشرب *mā' ash-shurb/li-sh-shurb* drinking water 6

مادّة موادّ *mādda mawādd* (also:) clause, article 7

ماش\الماشي *māshin (al-māshī)* going, proceeding 15

مال *māl* (sing., also:) wealth 4

مبرد مبارد *mibrad mabārid* file, rasp 2

مبيّضة *mubayyaḍa* fair copy 17

متتال\المتتالي *mutatālin, al-mutatālī* (weak) successive 18

متّحدة see برنامج

متزوّج *mutazawwij* married 3

متسلسل *mutasalsil* consecutive 7

متطرّف *mutaṭarrif* extreme, extremist 10

متعاطف مع *muta'āṭif ma'* sympathetic to 11

متوسّط see بحر

مثقب مثاقب *mithqab mathāqib* drill, bit 2

مجروح → مجارح

مجال *majāl* domain, range 12

مجتمع *mujtama'* society 3

مجروح مجاريح *majrūḥ majārīḥ* injured 6

مجلس إدارة *majlis 'idāra* board of directors 4

مجموع *majmū'* total 17

محاباة *muḥābā* favouritism 5

محادثة *muḥādatha* discussion 10

محاسبة *muḥāsaba* accounting 15

محاكمة *muḥākama* trial 7

محتويات *muḥtawayāt* (pl.) contents 17

محدود *maḥdūd* limited, Ltd. 4

محرّك *muḥarrik* engine 16

محطّة *maḥaṭṭa* stop, station 2

محمّد *muḥammad* Muhammad 3

محمود *maḥmūd* Mahmud 10

المحيط الأطلسي\الأطلنطي *al -muḥīṭ al-'aṭlasī/al-'aṭlanṭī* Atlantic Ocean 13

المحيط الهادي\الهندي *al-muḥīṭ al-hādī/al-hindī* Pacific/Indian Ocean 13

مختار مخاتير *mukhtār makhātīr*
mayor (of a village) 3

مخرج مخارج *makhraj makhārij*
exit 2

مخلص *mukhliṣ* sincere 15

مدّد *maddada* II extend
(something) 12

مدّعٍ\المدّعي *mudda'in,*
al-mudda'ī (weak) plaintiff,
prosecutor 7

(الـ)مدّعى عليه *mudda'an,*
al-mudda'a (weak) 'alayhi
defendant 7

مدخل مداخل *madkhal madākhil*
entrance 2

مدني *madanī* civil (case, law,
engineering etc.) 7

(الـ)مدى *madan (al-mada)*
extent 14

مذكّرة *mudhakkara*
memorandum 10

مذنب *mudhnib* guilty 7

إمرأة see المرأة

مربّع *murabba'* square(d) 17

مرشّح *murashshaḥ* (also:)
having a cold 6

مرشد *murshid* guide 14

مرض يمرض *maraḍa yamraḍu* I
fall ill 6

مرض أمراض *maraḍ 'amrāḍ*
disease 6

مرعيّ *mar'īy* complied with 10

مركز جماعي *markaz jamā'ī*
community centre 3

مريض مرضى *marīḍ marḍa*
sick 6

مريم *maryam* Mariam, Mary 15

مساحة *misāḥa* area 13

مسافة *masāfa* distance 16

مسمار → مسامير

مساهم *musāhim* shareholder 4

مساواة *musāwā* equality 12

مستحقّ (لـ) *mustaḥiqq (li-)*
deserving (of), eligible (for) 3

مستفيد *mustafīd* beneficiary 9

مستمع *mustami'* listener 10

مستند *mustanad* document,
record 17

مستوصف *mustawṣaf* clinic 2

مسح يمسح :مسح *masaḥa*
yamsaḥu I scan 15, wipe 16;
see آلة

مسلم *muslim* Muslim 3

مسمار مسامير *mismār masāmīr*
nail, rivet 2

مسوّدة *musawwada* draft 17

مسؤولية *mas'ūlīya* (also:)
liability 9

مسيحي *masīḥī* Christian 3

مشاهد *mushāhid* viewer 10

مشروب *mashrūb* drink 5

مضيق مضايق *maḍīq maḍāyiq*
strait 13

مطبخ مطابخ *miṭbakh maṭābikh*

stove, *maṭbakh maṭābikh* kitchen 2
مطر أمطار *maṭar 'amṭār* rain, تمطر السماء *tamṭur as-samā'* it is raining 13
مطعم مطاعم *maṭ'am maṭā'im* restaurant 2
مطّلع على *muṭṭáli' 'ala* aware of 11
مطلق *muṭlaq* absolute 11
معرض ← معارض
معاش (تقاعد) *ma'āsh (taqā'ud)* (retirement) pension 2
معالجة النصوص *mu'ālajat an-nuṣūṣ* wordprocessing 15
معتدل *mu'tádil* moderate 10
معتمد (إلى) *mu'támad ('ila)* accredited (to) 10
معدني *ma'dinī* mineral 5
معرض معارض *ma'riḍ ma'āriḍ* exhibition hall 2
معونة *ma'ūna* assistance 12
مفتاح مفاتيح *miftāḥ mafātīḥ* key, switch 2
مفرق مفارق *mafraq mafāriq* crossroad 2
مقابل *muqābil* remuneration 2
مقابلة *muqābala* interview 2
مقرّ ← مقارّ
مقاليد *maqālīd* (pl.) reins 14
مقياس ← مقاييس
مقتضى: بمقتضى *bi-muqtaḍa* in conformity with 12
مقرّ مقارّ *maqarr maqārr* headquarters 12
مقهى (الـ) *maqhan (al-maqha)* (weak), pl. مقاه\المقاهي *maqāhin (al-maqāhī)* (weak) coffee-house 2
مقياس مقاييس *miqyās maqāyīs* gauge, meter 2
مكنسة ← مكانس
مكعّب *muka''ab* cube(d), cubic 17
مكنسة مكانس *miknasa makānis* broom 2
ملحق ← ملاحق
ملعب ← ملاعب
ملعقة ← ملاعق
ملح أملاح *milḥ 'amlāḥ* (m./f.) salt 5
ملحق *mulḥaq* attaché, ملحق بحري\تجاري\ثقافي\للطيران\عسكري *mulḥaq baḥrī/tijārī/thaqāfī/li-ṭ-ṭayarān/'askarī* naval/commercial/cultural/air/military attaché 10
ملعب ملاعب *mal'ab malā'ib* stadium, playground 2
ملعقة ملاعق *mil'aqa malā'iq* spoon 5
ملك يملك *malaka yamliku* I own 9
ملك أملاك *milk 'amlāk* property 9
ملك ملوك *malik mulūk* king 11

ملكة *malika* queen 11
ملموس *malmūs* tangible 18
ملك ← ملوك
مملكة ← ممالك
ممثّل see مندوب
ممرّض\ممرّضة *mumarriḍ(a)* nurse 2
مملكة ممالك *mamlaka mamālik* kingdom 2
من *min* (also:) over (in fractions) 17
مناخ *munākh* climate 13
منديل ← مناديل
منزل ← منازل
منشار ← مناشر
منشف ← مناشف
مناقصة *munāqaṣa* call for tenders 5
منح يمنح *manaḥa yamnaḥu* I grant to 3
منح *manḥ* granting, award 3
مندوب\ممثّل (نقابة) عمّال :مندوب *mandūb/mumaththil (niqābat) 'ummāl* shop steward 2
منديل مناديل *mandīl manādīl* handkerchief 16
منزل منازل *manzil manāzil* residence 2
منشار مناشير *minshār manāshīr* saw 2
منشفة مناشف *minshafa manāshif* towel 2
منظّمة التحرير الفلسطينية *munaẓẓamat at-taḥrīr al-filasṭīnīya* Palestine Liberation Organisation, PLO 11
منظور *manẓūr* foreseeable 11
منقلب *munqálab* place of defeat 2
مهنة مهن *mihna mihan* (also:) career 2
مادّة ← موادّ
موعد ← مواعد
موقع ← مواقع
موانئ *mawāni'* ports 4
مؤسّسة *mu'assasa* institution 12
موعد مواعد *maw'id mawā'id* appointment 2
مؤقّت *mu'aqqat* temporary 4
موقع مواقع *mawqi' mawāqi'* site 5
مولّد *muwallid* generator 16
مؤلّف *mu'allaf* composed 14
مؤهّل *mu'ahhil* qualification, *mu'ahhal* qualified, skilled 2
ماء ← مياه
ميليار *mīliyār* milliard 5
مئوي: مئوية (درجة) *(daraja) mi'awīya* (degree) celsius 17

ن

نادر *nādir* rare 13
ناد\النادي أندية *nādin, an-nādī 'ándiya* (weak) club 3
ناشف *nāshif* dry 13
ناطق\ناطقة بلسان *nāṭiq(a) bi-lisān*

spokesman (-woman) 4
ناقص *nāqiṣ* (also:) minus 17
نتج ينتج *nataja yantiju* I result, follow, ... ينتج أنّ *yantij 'anna* ... it follows that ... 17
نجّار *najjār* carpenter 2
نجارة *nijāra* carpentry 2
نجم نجوم *najm nujūm* star 13
نسبة *nisba* relation(ship), proportion 17
نسخ ينسخ *nasakha yansakhu* I copy 15
نسل ينسل *nasala yansulu* I fray 16
إمرأة ← نسوان
نسيج أنسجة *nasīj 'ansija* texture 16
نشف *nashaf* dryness 13
نصح ينصح (ل ب) *naṣaḥa yanṣaḥu* I (*li*- person, *bi*- thing) advise 7
نصف *niṣf* semi-, bi- see 4/4; نصف أنصاف *niṣf 'anṣāf* half 14, 17
نظافة *niẓāfa* cleanness 6
نظام أنظمة *niẓām 'anẓima* regulation, rule 2
نظر أنظار *naẓar 'anẓār* view, consideration, نظراً إلى\ل *naẓaran 'ila/li-* in view of, with a view to 9
نظير ← نظراء
نظيف ← نظفاء
نظّف *naẓẓafa* II clean 6
نظّم *naẓẓama* II organise 4
نظير نظراء *naẓīr nuẓarā'* counterpart 10
نظيف نظفاء *naẓīf nuẓafā'* clean 6
نفّذ *naffadha* II implement 12
نفقة *nafaqa* expense 10
نفوذ *nufūdh* influence 11
نقابة عمّال *niqābat 'ummāl* trade union 2; see مندوب
نقّاش *naqqāsh* painter 2
نقاشة *niqāsha* painting 2
نقد نقود *naqd nuqūd* currency 14; see صندوق
نموذج *namūdhaj* model; form (document) 9
نهاية *nihāya* end; نهايةً\ في النهاية *nihāyatan/ fi n-nihāya* finally 11
نهائي *nihā'ī* final 12
نوّع *nawwa'a* II diversify 12
نوعًا ما *naw'an mā* somewhat, somehow 11
نيابة *niyāba* replacement, deputyship, نيابةً عن *niyābatan 'an* deputising for, in place of 9

ه

هاتف هواتف *hātif hawātif* (official lang.) telephone 10
محيط see هادي

هدف أهداف *hadaf 'ahdāf* goal 12

هدّد (ب) *haddada* II *(bi-)* threaten (with) 11

هرم أهرام *haram 'ahrām* pyramid 15

هما *huma* they both 5

هنّ *hunna* they (f. pl.) 5

هنّأ (على) *hanna'a* II *('ala)* congratulate (on) 15

هندي see محيط

هاتف ← هواتف

هيكل هياكل *haykal hayākil* structure, framework 4

هيئة *hay'a* group, body 4

و

واد\الوادي وديان *wādin, al-wādī widyān* (weak) valley 13

واط *wāṭ* watt 16

وافر *wāfir* abundant 15

وجع أوجاع *waja' 'awjā'* pain 6

وجع يوجع *waji'a yawja'u* I be painful, feel pain 6

وجه وجوه *wajh wujūh* face 13

وحدة *waḥda* unit 14

ودّ يودّ *wadda yawaddu* I want 18

واد ← وديان

وراء: إلى الوراء *'ila l-warā'* backwards 16

ورث يرث *waritha yarithu* I inherit 7

ورث *wirth* inheritance 7

وريث ورثاء *warīth wurathā'* heir 7

وزّع *wazza'a* II distribute 12

وساخة *wasākha* dirt 6

وسائل إعلام *wasā'il 'i'lām* publicity/news media 13

وسّخ *wassakha* II soil 6

وسخ *wasikh* dirty 6

الوسطى see عصور

وسع *wus'* capability 14

وصل يصل (ب) *waṣala yaṣilu* I *(bi-)* connect (to) 15

وفر يفر *wafara yafiru* I abound 15

وفق *wafq* conformity 9; وفقًا ل *wafqan li-* pursuant to, in accordance with 7, 9

وقّع (على) *waqqa'a* II *('ala)* impose (a penalty) (on) 7

وقود *wuqūd* fuel 16

ولادة *wilāda* birth 6

ي

يا *yā* vocative particle, see 10/6

يسار *yasār* left (not right) 9

يلي: ما يلي *mā yalī* what follows 17

يمين *yamīn* right (not left) 9

يهودي يهود *yahūdī yahūd* Jew(ish) 3

يوسف *yūsuf* Yusuf, Joseph 3

يومًا ما *yawman mā* one of these days 11

Grammatical Index

Figures refer to: Chapter no./paragraph no. The sign → refers to another entry in the Index.

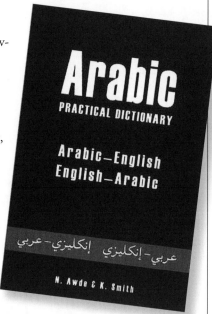

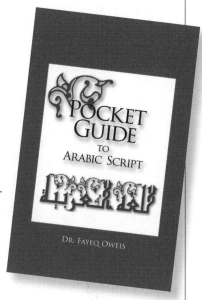

BASIC ARABIC WORKBOOK: FOR REVISION AND PRACTICE (pb)
John Mace

One of the foremost writers today of teaching materials for Middle Eastern languages, John Mace has now produced a key workbook for all learners of Modern Standard Arabic. Basic Arabic Workbook is a step by step series of exercises and tasks that puts the living standard language into practice using the most up-to-date vocabulary and situations, drawn from everyday situations, mainly the workplace. No previous knowledge is assumed beyond that of the alphabet.

Points of grammar and usage are clearly highlighted and explained throughout the workbook, making this also a handy reference work. Particular attention is paid to building vocabulary—reaching a total of approximately 1,300 words—accompanied by a clear transliteration of the Arabic script to aid pronunciation and stress. Apart from its approach, which is a first for Arabic, the book contains many other helpful features including a key to the exercises, indexes of the vocabulary and grammar, and an appendix with tables. Exercises avoid translation and consist of manipulation within the language, encouraging the student to think in Arabic and to highlight alternative structures. The nightmare of the numbers is avoided by using the now universal simplified form. This is the perfect tool for any taught or self-study Arabic language course.

352 PAGES • 6 X 9 • 0-7818-1126-0 • W • $29.95pb

ARABIC-ENGLISH/ENGLISH-ARABIC DICTIONARY & PHRASEBOOK
Jane Wightwick & Mahmoud Gaafar

As the national language of nearly 20 countries in Africa and Asia, and spoken by approximately 190 million people, Arabic is the lingua franca of the Middle East. This title uses a standard Arabic helpful to those traveling all over the region. The emphasis is on commonly heard terms and phrases that are recognizable throughout the Arabic-speaking world. Both the dictionary and phrasebook incorporate the Arabic script and its romanized transliteration. The two-way dictionary contains important travel, geographical, and cultural terminology, while the phrasebook focuses on the needs of the traveler and covers almost every situation from arrival to departure.

250 pages • 3¾ x 7½ • 3,000 entries • $12.95pb • ISBN: 0-7818-0973-8

WESTERN ARMENIAN-WNGLISH/ENGLISH-WESTERN ARMENIAN DICTOINARY & PHRASEBOOK
Nicholas Awde & Vazken-Khatchig Davidian

Western Armenian is the language spoken by most of the seven million Diaspora Armenians who live outside their historic homeland. Western Armenian speakers from the majority of Armenian spoken in the United States, Iran, and the Middle East. The language has helped to preserve a unified Armenian sense of identity and common cultural heritage throughout the world. This Dictionary and Phrasebook, an extension of that cultural heritage, offers insight into the historical roots of the Diaspora and provides and invaluable reference to the language itself. The book contains a resourceful two-way dictionary, an informative grammar section, and a collection of travel-oriented phrases. Armenian has its own unique alphabet, but to facilitate pronunciation, this book uses a common sense Roman transliteration system.

175 pages • 3¾ x 7½ • 3,000 entries • ISBN: 0-7818-1048-5 • $11.95pb

THE ARAB WORLD: AN ILLUSTRATED HISTORY
Kirk H. Sowell

This account presents a panoramic view of the history of the Arab peoples, whose world has expanded from the Arabian Peninsula to include North Africa, the Levant, and the Persian Gulf. The narrative depicts the rise of Islam, the life of the Prophet Muhammad, and the empire founded by his successors, which encompassed the Middle East, North Africa, and Spain. Following this empire's fragmentation circa A.D. 900, Central Asian rulers controlled the Arab world. Ultimately, the age of European dominance produced the modern Middle Eastern and North African states. The author concludes with an analysis of present-day challenges facing the Arab states.

235 pages • 5½ x 8½ • b/w photos/illus/maps • ISBN: 0-7818-0990-8 • $14.95pb

FARSI-ENGLISH/ENGLISH-FARSI DICTIONARY & PHRASEBOOK Romanized
Nicholas Awde, Asmatullah Sarwan & Camilla Shahribaf

Farsi, or Persian, is the official language of Iran, where more than half of the 67 million people speak the language. Farsi is now written in a form of the Arabic script called Perso-Arabic, but it is presented here in a romanized, easy-to-use form for instant communication. This volume uses the Tehran standard of Farsi. In addition to a pronunciation guide and transliteration system of the Farsi alphabet, the book contains a resourceful two-way dictionary, an informative grammar section, and a collection of travel-oriented phrases. Observations related to travel and culture are also interspersed throughout the phrasebook.

240 pages •3¾ x 7½ • 4,000 entries • ISBN: 0-7818-1073-6 • $ 11.95pb

BEGINNER'S IRAQI ARABIC WITH 2 Audio CDs
Nawal Nasrallah and Nadia Hassani

This introduction to the spoken language of Iraq is suitable for classroom use and self-study. It is designed both for people with no previous knowledge of the Arabic language and those who know some Arabic and wish to learn the Iraqi dialect. The foundation of the book is a series of realistic dialogues that increase in complexity with each lesson. The language is based on the Baghdadi dialect, which is understood by a majority of Iraqis. All Arabic words are transliterated into roman script for easy understanding. New vocabulary is explained prior to each dialogue, while additional vocabulary related to the topic is also provided. The grammar, expressions, and cultural material found in the dialogues are fully explained in their proper context.

The grammar is also presented in a logical, step-by-step manner for easy mastery. Each unit is supplemented with exercises that test and reinforce the student's knowledge, with an answer key provided at the end of the book. The two-way glossary contains more than 5,000 entries, enabling the book to double as a dictionary for travelers to Iraq. An audio CD feature accompanies the lessons.

250 pages • 5½ x 8½ • 2 80-minute audio CDS • ISBN: 0-7818-1098-1 • $29.95pb

MASTERING ARABIC WITH AUDIO CDS
Jane Wightwick & Mahmoud Gaafar

Now on audio CDs and repackaged! Each of the 19 chapters of Mastering Arabic, which covers the Modern Standard language is presented on two 60-minute compact discs.

370 pages • 6 x 9 • two 60 minute audio CDs • $29.95pb • ISBN: 0-7818-1042-6

A HISTORY OF THE ISLAMIC WORLD
Fred James Hill & Nicholas Awde

This concise depiction of the Islamic world features developments from the time of Muhammad and the rise of Islam in the seventh century to the complex political map of today. It clearly outlines and explains the major periods of Islam's phenomenal development and growth worldwide by focusing on the religious, cultural, and political achievements of the great Islamic Empires, including the golden age of the Abbasids in Baghdad, the Turkish Ottomans, and the Mughals of India. The book also features a chapter on medieval Muslim Spain. Special boxed sections provide informative snapshots of Islamic culture such as development of the Arabic language, architecture, and poetry. Included are more than 50 illustrations and maps.

224 pages • 5½ x 8½ • W •50 b/w photos/illus/maps • ISBN: 0-7818-1015-9 • $22.50hc